Wake

It's Never Too Late

Hernando Salcedo-Phillips, M.D.

Wake Up – It's Never Too Late

By Hernando Salcedo-Phillips, MD.

First Edition

ISBN-13: 978-1723086182

ISBN 10: 1723086185

Dedication

This book is dedicated with gratitude and appreciation to all men and women past and present who have been courageous enough to think and act "outside the box".

To Ana Cristina Moreno, the love of my life,

To my son Andres Julian Salcedo,

To my grandson Ayden Jasper Salcedo.

Acknowledgements

I would like to acknowledge Andres Salcedo for the graphic design work on the cover of this book.

I would also like to acknowledge Malcom Massey for his assistance as Independent Publishing Consultant to help get my book ready for publication.

Introduction

My long medical career ended last year, when I retired from the private practice of Urology. I was 78 years old, and it was then that I decided to write this book. I had thought about writing it several times before, but not until my retirement did I have the time and the will to do it.

As I look back over my years of my medical practice, I realize that I had many interesting experiences, such as witnessing miraculous healings, listening to patients describe to me in detail their near death experiences, and learning that the patient's beliefs had a great impact on how they respond to medical treatment. The notion that the mind has great influence on the body is something that I had the opportunity to confirm time and time again.

One of the most important lessons learned is that our thoughts create the world we experience and that the world we see and touch that we hold so dear is nothing but illusion, and nothing else.

These experiences opened my mind and made me question the very nature of reality and to consider the possible existence of worlds that are beyond the scope of our vision. I developed great hunger for the truth, and that lead me to many disciplines including

the Rosicrucian teachings, Silva Mind
Control seminars, both basic and advanced,
EST, Dr. Douglas Baker's seminars, several
types of meditation, study of a course in
Miracles for several years, seminars at the
Monroe Institute in Virginia, many courses
on self-awareness, and literally hundreds of
books on self-improvement, hypnosis,
esoteric sciences, and eastern philosophies.

I felt that the lessons I had learned were
very significant and that they should be
shared, as they may assist the readers on
their learning process.

I do not consider myself an expert on any of
the subjects in this book, I just would like
to spark the curiosity of my readers and
fire in them the desire to learn more about
what is covered in this writing, open their
minds, and invite them to ponder on the
truth behind the notions that we create our
own reality, and that the world we see and
touch is nothing but illusion, so that they
can make up their own minds as what is real
and what is not. I do not expect the reader
to accept everything that is written. It is
however the truth, as I have investigated
it, and this is an effort to share that
truth. To this effect, I embarked in the
production of this work.

I am aware that many fine books have written
on the subjects covered, and I would like to
invite the reader to study them, gain more

knowledge, and further expand their curiosity and interest.

In the first part of the book, I mention experiences that I had which made a big impact in my life. Subsequent chapters deal with practical subjects such as meditation, the mind body connection, the holographic world, the new science and other themes of importance.

The last chapter is dedicated to what the new world shall be like, given the significant changes what we are seen in all aspects of life; political, spiritual, in education, science, and medicine, to mention but a few.

Even though we have made great advances in technology, science, and have witnessed incredible advances in the medical field, we lag behind when it comes to answering the basic human questions such as who we really are, why we are here, what is our next step in our evolution, is there life after death, and other significant questions.

The ancient philosophers thought that our first priority should be to know ourselves and discover who we really are behind our personalities. Deep within all of us is the answer to all our questions and solution to our problems.

Table of Contents

Chapter 1

My Earlier experiences

It was in my last year of high school that I was exposed to a book "The Magic of Belief" written by Claude M. Bristol. It impacted me in ways that I did not understand at the time. The main point of the book was that visualization was the key to creating what we really want in our lives. It explained how by making a mental picture of what we want and keeping it in mind, it would eventually become reality. It contained several examples of cases in real life to make it compelling and believable. Although I found the book very interesting, I did not try to use the visualization technique until I was in medical school a few years later.

In my first year of medical school, anatomy was a subject that was feared by students as it was used as a filter to the advancement to the next course. Failing this subject would put you in great disadvantage and threatened you to the possibility expulsion from the school.
The anatomy professor Dr. Barrientos was a wise old man, very respected for his knowledge but who did not have a very nice

personality.

He frequently used tricks in the exams, like cutting little windows on the skin of the wrists of the cadavers, and then turning them on their abdomen, so that it was difficult to get oriented, and then pick on nerves, arteries etc., and then demand from the students the names of those structures. This was frequently difficult as they all looked similar and of the same color on a dead body, because of the formaldehyde injected to preserve them.

One day while doing a dissection on a body, he had some difficulty isolating a nerve, because he had a small hand tremor, and I made the mistake of trying to help him. He raised his thick eyebrows, looked at me over his black rim glasses hanging half way on his nose and gave me a disapproving, dirty look. He then said. "Thank you," said Don Olegario when he was thrown out of his horse, "I was just ready to get off."

After this episode, I always had the feeling that he did not like me very much and from that time on, I was afraid that he would fail me in the final exam, something that would be catastrophic.

As time went by, my anxiety level increased, and it was then that I remember the Bristol's book on visualization. If it was true that visualization created the reality we wanted, would it be possible to visualize a happy year ending having approved all the subjects including the anxiety producing anatomy? I thought about it for a while, and decided to give it a try. Could the visualization really help me? Could this be true? I remember the examples in the book, and decided that after all, I had nothing to lose.

I started making a mental picture of the professor in the final exam, smiling at me, asking questions about the anatomy of the chest; an area in which I felt more confident. I visualized myself being calmed, self-assured, and answering questions with ease. I even visualized him congratulating me on having passed the exam, (which was unheard of him, ever having done that to any student) and other details as to how I wanted the exam to go.

I set up to practice the mental image for about twenty minutes every day, week after week to the point where my confidence level was significantly improved.

The day of the final exam arrived. It was, as I recall, a cold rainy morning. As I entered the large examining room in the morgue, there were many students, all nervous, awaiting their names to be called in alphabetical order. I was one of the last ones on the student list, and that meant more stress time.

Dr. Barrientos did not appear as grouchy as

usual, and to my great surprise he started
the exam by asking me questions on the
anatomy of the chest (just as I had
visualized). After this, the rest of the
exam became easier. I was confident, and at
the end, he did not congratulate me as I had
envisioned, but had a grin in his face I had
never seen before, and gave me what I
interpreted as a look of approval.
The next day I went to look at the list of
the final grades, and was very pleased with
my more than passing grade.
Whether the visualization exercises helped
me or not I will never know, but one thing
was certain, it gave me confidence in this
technique to awaken my continued interest in
it.

I did not use the visualization technique
again until half way through medical school.
I heard from a friend that there was a great
opportunity of working as a nurse, during
the year-end vacation in one of the cargo
ships of the Grancolombiana Merchant Fleet.
This was a Colombian fleet of large ships
that transported cargo to Europe, North, and
South America. This opportunity, I thought,
would be great for me, as it would give me a
chance to visit several countries, see the
sea and get on a ship for the first time
ever. I was living in Bogota, Colombia, a
city away from the coast and I had seen the
ocean only in movies.

I quickly checked the schedules of the fleet, but the only trip that I could take during the year-end vacation was in the "City of Medellin" ship, scheduled to leave port on Nov 9th.

The problem was that my final exams would not end until Nov 15th. I could not possibly risk not taking those last exams for it would mean failing them. The other problem was that I did not know anything about nursing. One learns in medical school to diagnose and treat illnesses but I did not know how to give an injection or do the basic nursing procedures.

These appear to be insurmountable obstacles, but I was so excited about the possibility of the trip, that I was thinking about it day and night, almost to the exclusion of all else.

I started to hang around nurses in the hospital, to learn from them the basics. But the main drawback was that the final exams of surgery, preventive medicine, and internal medicine, were scheduled to take place after November 9th, the day the ship was scheduled to depart.

One morning I woke up with the idea of the possibility of having those tests given to me alone in advance, before the scheduled time. This would not appear very likely, as I would have to go to each of the teachers and ask them to make an exception to the

rule, something that to my knowledge, had
never been done before.

I was so excited about the job though, that
I would have done anything possible to get
it. It was then that the visualization
technique I had learned before came to my
rescue. I immediately started visualizing
just like the book taught. Very frequently
during the day I would close my eyes and see
myself in my mind working in the ship, in
white uniform, talking to the members of the
crew, enjoying the trip and performing every
aspect of what I thought the job was about.
I became obsessed with the trip and few
weeks later decided to speak to the
professors giving the tests to ask them for
their help as I was determined to try my
luck.

I called Doctor Andrade, the surgeon
responsible for the surgery test and made an
appointment to see him at his office, not
telling the receptionist the true reason for
my visit, for fear of being rejected. A few
days later, I went to see him at his office.
He had a reputation for being a great
surgeon and had a very large practice. I had
to wait some half an hour to see him.
Dr. Andrade was a huge man with nice
demeanor and presence. His office was
beautifully decorated and had a very
professional look. I felt confident, and did
not feel intimidated, just as I had
rehearsed it in my mind, over and over

again.

After greeting me with a smile, he asked me what seemed to be the problem. As planned, I told him the real reason for being there. I must have made my desperate plead clear, for he did not ask any questions, just called his secretary to bring him his appointment book and said: "Can you come next Monday? I can give you the test at 6:00 pm after my last patient appointment." This first meeting took place just as I had pictured it in my mind.

I was there on the appointed Monday, a good half an hour before the scheduled time. I felt confident and ready to go. He asked me to take a seat and make myself comfortable. He then said: "Tell me all you know about acute diverticulitis, what causes it, how do you diagnose it, how do you treat it, what are the possible complications, and how can you avoid further recurrence. If I am satisfied with your answers there will be no further questions."

I proceeded to answer his many questions and at the end, he told me I had passed and that he would make sure that the grade would be placed on my file. He then wished me well and good luck in my trip.

I was ecstatic, to say the least. The first hurdle was being removed.

I could hardly believe I had pulled this through. It gave me the confidence to consider requesting the other two professors

for their test in advance.   Unlike the
first exam which went so well, the other two
were not as easy. The physician in charge of
preventive medicine was reluctant to do it
and sounded very discouraging. It was not
until I explained to him that there had been
a precedent and that Dr. Andrade had already
anticipated my test, that he reluctantly
agreed to do it.

In the meantime, the merchant company was
pressing me to sign a contract, as the time
of departure was getting close. Although, I
was not quite ready, I signed it and took my
chances with the remaining final tests.

The preventive medicine professor gave me a
passing grade. All I had to do now was to
study day and night to pass the last test
which was internal medicine, the one I
considered the most difficult. When the time
came, I was nervous, but felt confident, and
I managed to answer most of the questions
well, despite the fact that they were not
easy and that the professor was not in the
best of moods, obviously, by having to take
extra time from his busy schedule to do
something he had never done before. Having
passed this last examination, my excitement
increased, I felt on top of the world, and
started to learn as much as I could about
those countries I was about to visit.

I don't know to what extent my visualization
exercises worked, but as in the case of the
anatomy examination, it gave me the

necessary confidence required to request the
tests in advance, and talk those doctors
into making an exception to the rule.
Having removed the last obstacle, I made the
required arrangements for the trip. I
obtained a passport, and I was ready to go.
I flew to Buenaventura, located at the west
coast of Colombia, the port of departure. I
got there two days ahead of time because I
did not want to take any chances of any last
minute mishaps.
The city was very hot and humid. Most of the
population there are of African descent, and
I had seen a black person before, only
occasionally. I felt somewhat intimidated at
first by their huge size as most of them
were well over 6 feet tall.
The day before the scheduled departure I
visited the harbor. I had never seen the sea
before, left alone ships of any size.
I was very excited. The "City of Medellin"
in which I was to embark was an 18,000 ton
ship neatly painted and it looked
impressive. The next day, I boarded the
ship, went through all the check in routine,
and to my pleasant surprise, as I had
visualized so many times, I was assigned a
place at the captain's table. Everything was
new to me, it was totally a new experience.
I felt a degree of excitement which I had
never experienced before. The ship left the
harbor in early afternoon. The sound of the
ship's horn as it left port is still present

in my memory as if I had heard it yesterday.
To say that I was elated would be an
understatement. The ship sailed to Ecuador,
Peru, and then and then back north to
Buenaventura, Colombia, the port of
departure. We then sailed north, through the
Panama Canal. The passage through the canal
was quite an interesting experience. The
Gatun Lake which is half way though the
canal is higher than the oceans, and several
locks have to be filled so the ships can get
through.
We then sailed through the wavy Caribbean,
to the Gulf of Mexico in route to the
southern coast of the United States. We
visited Galveston, Houston, Port Arthur and
then New Orleans.
After a layover in New Orleans of three
days, we left on Nov 23rd which was the day
of my 21st birthday. It was about 7:00 pm
when the ship left the harbor. The sun was
just going down over the horizon, casting
the most spectacular sunset I had ever
experienced. The lights of the city created
a breathtaking view. It was then, that I
decided to come back to the United States to
do my specialty after finishing medical
school,a decision that I stood by and
carried out.

Barichara A pocketful of miracles

In Colombia, after a student finishes medical school and serves a year of internship, it is required of him to do one year of rural medicine work, before he can obtain his MD degree.

I chose Barichara, a beautiful small town of 7,000 people, white painted houses with blue-green doors and windows, and streets paved with symmetrically placed large slab stones.

The hospital was a one floor white building, with a lovely central garden immaculately trimmed, surrounded by patients rooms. It was very well managed by nuns who kept it running like a clock.

Mother Teresa was the administrator of the Hospital. She was a remarkable nun in her early sixties always with a pleasant smile. When you were in front of her you could not help feeling that you were in the presence of a great soul.

She gave me a warm welcome. I was the only physician in town and my new position was as medical director of the hospital.

She enjoyed being a surgical assistant but was frustrated because the doctor I was replacing did not do any surgery and she was

11

very pleased to know that I was also interested in the surgical field.

The hospital had many investments and properties, so that the income it generated was much larger than the expenses, and knowing this, I handed Mother Teresa a long list of surgical instruments and gadgets we would need to restore the operating room, which she was only too happy to accept.

Shortly after I arrived, one day on Christmas Eve, I got a phone call from Mother Teresa. She had just received notice that there was a pregnant woman in a remote village, who had been bleeding for several days and was very ill. She was being brought to the hospital by her husband on a horse cart, as there were no roads to the village. Mother Teresa said she would call me as soon as the patient arrived.

Some two hours later the call came. After rushing to the hospital I found the patient to be in extremely poor condition, she looked as though she were dead already. She was comatose, very pale and cold, with no blood pressure, palpable pulse, or any other signs of life, except for an occasional shallow breath, and a sluggish weak pupil response to light. There was no fetal heart beat which indicated to me that the fetus was dead. She had persistent vaginal bleeding. I calculated the pregnancy to be about eight months.

With this somber clinical picture, the only
thing to do was to perform an emergency
cesarean section in an attempt to stop the
bleeding and hopefully to save whatever life
was still there.
Since she was unconscious, there was no
point in giving her any spinal anesthesia,
the only anesthesia that was available to us
at the time.
We gave her all life support we could give
her, and took her quickly to the operating
room. At that time we had not received the
equipment for the type and cross match of
blood required for transfusions, so there
was no way we could give her any blood.
She continued to be unconscious with no
evidence of blood pressure or pulse. I
opened her abdomen, then opened the uterus,
and extracted the dead fetus and the
placenta. The bleeding however persisted,
and no amount of stitching would stop it.
At this point sister Ana the nun in charge
of the OR said: "Doctor, the blood that has
fallen on the floor is not clotting." It was
then that I realized that a fatal
complication had developed. It was called
"consumption coagulopathy," a serious toxic
condition in which the blood does not clot
and bleeding cannot be stopped. I look at
the wall of the uterus that was opened and
saw what is called the rainbow sign, the
wall of the uterus appeared as if made of
different layers, giving the appearance of a

rainbow, typical of this fatal complication. With this realization, there was nothing else for me to do. I proceeded to close the uterus, did not see any point in closing the abdominal wall, but limited myself to closing the skin, for I did not want to deliver to her husband the body of his wife with an open wound. I took my gloves and gown off, and I was done!

I was surprised when Mother Teresa who had been the first assistant during the procedure asked me for postoperative orders. Mother, I said, "This patient is dead! There is nothing I or anybody else can do. Whatever little bit of blood she had is gone."
"You have no faith," Mother Teresa exclaimed. "She is a beautiful child of God."
"Come on, Mother!" I said, with exasperation in my voice. "If this lady survives I will give up medicine, because everything I have learned is false."
I left the hospital shortly after that to enjoy a Christmas Eve dinner with the town's pharmacist and his family.
The next morning I went to the hospital around 11 a.m. Mother Teresa greeted me at the door as usual. This time she had a strange grin on her face.
"At what time did you pronounce the patient dead last night?" I asked.

14

"Oh! She said, "I told you, you have no faith, let me show you something." She then took me to the patient's room.

I found the patient sitting up in bed having breakfast!!

I could not believe what I was seeing, I thought this was a different patient and left the room. Mother Teresa followed me and said: "This is Rosa, the patient you operated on last night."

She took me by my arm back into the room. "Good morning, Doctor," Rosa said. Mother Teresa told me what happened. I then pulled down her lower eyelid and saw a red conjunctiva, indicative of good blood flow, her skin was warm, and she had a normal strong pulse. I looked at the monitor hooked to her arm, her blood pressure was 120/85! Not believing what I was seeing I pulled down her covers and saw the surgical wound, and to my surprise, it was just like I had left it the night before. The patient had materialized out of thin air 9-10 pints of blood and had come back to life!

I was too young and too inexperienced to fully appreciate the miracle I had just witnessed. I remembered from the night before that Mother Teresa never thought that the patient would die. Quite the contrary, the thought of Rosa not surviving, never crossed her mind. She had just created a miracle, which was far from my comprehension.

The next day, I had to take Rosa back to the operating room, and under spinal anesthesia, closed the abdomen adequately. In those days it was the custom to leave patients in the hospital until the sutures from the skin were removed, one week later. At the end of the week, Rosa left the hospital with her husband, radiant, happy, and healthy as though nothing had happened.

Some two or three weeks later, on a Friday afternoon as I was preparing to spend the weekend in my hometown Bucaramanga about three hour drive away, the pharmacist came over to my office with the news that a twelve year old boy had come to his pharmacy complaining of abdominal pain.
I told the pharmacist what to give him and asked him to send the boy to the next town an hour away, if the pain did not subside.

I came back on Sunday night and went directly to the pharmacist house to find out about the boy. The pain did not stop he said, it got worse but I could not locate his parents and he had no way to leave town, so I took him to the hospital.
Alarmed, I rushed to the hospital. The boy's abdomen was rigid, indicative of severe peritonitis, a life threatening condition which requires immediate surgery. He had a high fever and there was nothing for me to do but to take him to surgery immediately.

16

As mentioned earlier, the only form of
anesthesia available to us was spinal, we
did not have general anesthesia equipment,
and of course no anesthesiologist. I had
never given a child spinal anesthesia, and I
did not even know if it was possible, but I
was alone, there was nobody to ask, and I
just had to do it.
I figured out the dose of the anesthetic and
gave him the spinal. After a few tense
moments I was able to confirm that the
anesthesia had worked.
After giving him a massive dose of
antibiotics, I opened the abdomen, and found
the appendix very inflamed, stocked to
adjacent tissues, it had separated from the
colon leaving a hole in it. This was a
serious condition; perforated appendicitis.
I carefully closed the hole in the colon,
but there was not much else I could do. The
appendix was so stock to adjacent tissues
that any attempt at separating it would only
cause significant bleeding. I left large
drainage tubes as was the recommended thing
to do in those cases, and closed the wound.

The next morning, I had patients in the
office, so it was noon time before I was
able to go to the hospital. What I found as
I entered the hospital was shocking to say
the least. The boy whom I had just operated
on the night before was on the central patio
playing hopscotch, just like nothing had

happened the night before.

He had a marvelous recovery. It is true that children at that age recover much faster than adults, but this recovery was totally out of the ordinary, clearly another miracle of Mother Theresa.

When I spoke to her about it, she just smiled and said: "To God nothing is impossible."

There were other remarkable cures, not as striking as the two mentioned but definitely out of the ordinary. During my period of time working in that hospital nobody ever died.

Today, I would have asked Mother Teresa a million questions, but again, back then, I was too young and too inexperienced to really appreciate the miracles I had witnessed firsthand.

How could a patient like Rosa who had no chance of living made such an astonishing recovery? How could she have materialized 10 units of blood out of thin air? My mind was going in circles, completely baffled, not able to understand any of that.

Mother Teresa continued to do her duties and routine chores as though nothing out of the ordinary had happened, completely untouched by the miraculous events that to me were enough to shake my sense of reality.

I was left scratching my head in disbelief. The only possible explanation that I could come up with was that the incredible, unwavering faith of Mother Teresa had produced the miracles.

After I left town to do further studies in United States, I never saw Mother Teresa again, but the memory of that remarkable saint has always been and will always be with me.

My trip to the United States

Since I had decided to do my specialty in the US, I had to take the ECFMG (Educational Council for Foreign Medical Graduates) a test that was required for any graduates from a foreign medical school. If you passed the test you would qualify to train in US hospitals as if you had studied there.

In October of that year I traveled to Cali, a city in Colombia where the test was being offered. I took the four hour test and went back to Barichara the next day.
Two months later I received the good news that I had passed the exam and qualified to apply to any US hospital for further training. After filling out a few applications, I chose Piedmont Hospital in Atlanta, GA, and signed a contract to start

a year of internship on July 1, 1963. I made arrangements to fly to Miami, FL where I planned to stay overnight and then fly to Atlanta the next day.

I arrived at the airport in Miami, on June 18th. After clearing customs, I picked up my two suitcases and briefcase and went out to a telephone booth to book a hotel room for the night. Once I found a hotel, I went back inside the airport to have a cup of coffee before going downtown where the hotel was located. As I was ready to leave, I noticed to my bewilderment that I had the two suitcases but the briefcase containing all my papers, passport and money was not around. I looked about but could not see it anywhere. I knew I had it at the telephone boot when I made the phone call, but nearly a half an hour had gone by since I made that call and I was a long block away. An eerie feeling swept over my body.
I searched my pockets and all could find was two dollars. In total desperation, I decided to go back to the telephone booth. It was very hot, I was sweating profusely not so much from the heat but probably from the panic I was experiencing. The idea of being in a foreign country with a foreign language, with no papers, no passport or identity, no money, and not knowing anyone in town, was more than I could bear.

What would the chances be of finding it, I

asked myself. The street was very crowded and the booth was a long block away. In those days suitcases had no wheels, so, I picked them up and started to walk as fast as I could. I was hyperventilating, my heart pounding fast, and my legs felt weak. It was as though time stood still as I thought I'd never get there.

On my way, the miracles I experienced in Barichara, flashed through my mind as well as what Mother Teresa told me one time: when all seems lost, "the presence" comes to you and will solve your problem, but you have to believe in it, it is the faith that moves mountains. I thought about it with great hope, as I thought it would take one of those miracles to find it.

This was a situation where I was about to lose everything. Could the "presence" she was talking about really help me in this case? I quickly dismissed the thought, probably to avoid further frustration should I not find the briefcase.

At long last I found myself in front of the phone booth.

The door was closed, and I knew I had left it open. That meant that someone had already been at the booth, and that increased me stress level. I was frozen with fear.

Making a superhuman effort, I finally opened the door. My soul returned to my body, as by the phone, there was my briefcase, untouched, with everything in it. I don't remember how many times I kissed it. At last, I got my composure and headed to the hotel.

Although I would not consider this a miracle, I thought of it as a very happy occurrence, one that made me think that there is always hope when there doesn't appear to be any.

My non-physical experience

It was several years later, after I completed my specialty In Urology at the George Washington University Hospital in Washington DC, that this extraordinary experience took place, in Alexandria, VA, a suburb of Washington where I was living. It was on a Friday afternoon. I had just came home after a long day of urological procedures at the hospital. As usual, I lay in bed and closed my eyes to rest for a few minutes. All of a sudden, I was involved by a most brilliant white light, like a thousand suns coming from above and towards the left. This extraordinary light did not cast any shadows and it did not bother my eyes. The light constituted my very essence as I felt no separation from it, the light and I were one.

I was so stunned by this strange experience

that I felt as though my mind had just
stopped thinking. I knew I was not asleep, I
was fully conscious, but I had no thoughts.
I experience infinite love. A type of love I
had never experienced before. I had the
feeling that I knew everything, so much so
that it did not occur to me to use this
knowledge to think of a solution to my
present problems. I was One with everything,
and I was everywhere at the same time. If I
thought of a tree, there was no separation
between me and the tree, I was the tree. It
was an ecstatic experience. I reached a
state of indescribable peace and bliss. It
was beyond anything I had ever experienced
and beyond my ability to fully describe it
in words. I felt that I was not my body or
my personality, I existed, but not in
physical form, just pure infinite
consciousness, at one with all it is.

I don't know how long this experience
lasted, for time stood still, it could have
just five minutes, or may be an hour, time
simply did not exist.
After this experience ended, I remained in
bed, wide awake, unable to move, totally
transfixed by what had just taken place.
I knew I had not been asleep, the experience
had not been in my imagination, and it was
not a hallucination either.

I have never been able to duplicate this
experience, and nothing similar has happened

to me again. Since then I have read of
similar experiences reported by spiritually
evolved individuals and sages of Tibet,
India and other places. What I do not
understand is why I had that experience, as
I considered myself far from being a
spiritually advanced individual.
These were the experiences that made me look
further, and deeper into what reality is
beyond the physical appearance.

Chapter 2

The Holographic Universe

Today nearly everyone is familiar with holograms. Holograms are incredible three dimensional images projected into space with the aid of a laser. A hologram is produced when a single laser light is split in two separate beams. The first beam bounces off the object to be photographed, the second beam then collides with the reflected light of the first. When this happens an interference pattern is created which is recorded on a film. A three dimensional image is created which is very real looking, and this is what makes it so fascinating. It is so real looking that you can walk around the picture and view it from different angles as if it were a real three dimensional object, but if you try to touch it your hand will go right through it and then you realize that all is there is just an illusion and nothing else. This creates an incredible experience because it looks very real, yet you know it is really not there, it is an illusion.

There is however another aspect of a

hologram. The three dimensional illusion is not the only remarkable aspect of holograms. If a holographic film containing an image of an object, let's say a cat, is cut in half and then illuminated by a laser, each half will still be found to contain the entire image of the cat! If the halves are divided again and again, no matter how many times, when you shine a laser on them, each portion of the film will give a smaller picture of the whole entire cat. Unlike regular photographs, every small fragment of a piece of holographic film contains all the information contained in the whole.

The concept that the universe in which we live is a hologram, preposterous as it seemed, was first considered by two of the world's best known and recognized researchers: Karl Pribram, a neurophysiologist at Stanford University and author of the classic textbook "Languages of the Brain" and University of London physicist David Bohm who was one of the most respected quantum physicists.
Curiously enough, they both arrived at the same conclusion independently, out of frustration in their own fields of work. Bohm became convinced of the holographic nature of the universe after years of dissatisfaction and frustration from his inability to explain all the phenomena encountered in quantum physics.

Pribram was convinced of the holographic nature of the brain after many years of dissatisfaction with standard theories of the brain which had failed to explain neurological activities.

To him, this consideration was very exciting because it offered him a way of understanding how memories could be distributed rather than localized in the brain, which was the accepted view at the time.

It was possible for every part of the brain to contain all the information necessary for memory to occur since it had been shown that every portion of a holographic film contained all the information of the whole subject being photographed.

These two scientists putting their careers on the line, and facing severe opposition from their peers who were trained in the Newtonian model of physics, were courageous enough to go forth with their theory which would give them answers in their own fields of research, not otherwise found.

Both of these researchers soon realized that the holographic model would also help them explain a number of other elusive phenomena such as out of body and near death experiences, precognition, lucid dreams, ESP, miracles, psychokinesis, (the ability to move objects using the mind alone) and many other paranormal abilities of the mind. According to Bohm the separation of consciousness and matter is an illusion as consciousness and matter are one and the same.

Bohm and Pribram's theories provide a significant new way of looking at the world. They concluded that our brains construct objective reality by interpreting frequencies that are beyond space and time. Scientists had been unable to locate the area of the brain that contains all the memory because what we called memory exists according the holographic theory throughout the brain and body, and not in just one location. This theory also explains why people with brain tumors who have large parts of their brains removed, do not lose specific memories.

They both realized that the objective solid world that we hold so dear, does not really exist, at least not in the way we are used to believe it.

Pribram realized that what is "out there" is nothing but a vast ocean of waves and frequencies, with no solid reality, and that it looks solid only because our brains take this holographic model and decodes it into what to us appears as solid objects such as mountains, rocks, buildings and other familiar seeming solid objects which make our visible world.

Danish physicist Niels Bohr and David Bohm say that every part is an expression of the one invisible whole. Many great scientists are saying the same.

In the words of William Blake:

To see the World in a Grain of Sand

And a Heaven in a Wild Flower

Hold infinity in the palm of your

Hand and Eternity in an hour.

Fred Alan Wolf, Ph.D. Author of "Taking the Quantum Leap" and other important publications agrees with the idea of a holographic Universe, stating that the concept of the universe as a giant hologram, and the concept of consciousness and matter as a single field, would answer the questions of what reality is.

On a first sight the notion that the three dimensional objects that we see, touch and think real are nothing but holograms, seemed preposterous, and not readily accepted by the scientific community, but significant evidence is surfacing to support the hypothesis. In The Law of One series we are told that the Universe is one mind, that each one of us is a perfect holographic reflection of the one infinite creator. Michael Talbot, author of "Mysticism and the

New Physics," and "Beyond the Quantum,"
wrote a magnificent book "The Holographic
Universe," one of the most significant
scientific books written in modern times,
which gives us details of the new concept of
reality, and open one's mind and imagination
as to what is possible, what is reality and
what is illusion.[1]
This brilliant work discusses phenomena for
which no explanation has been satisfactory.
The idea that human body is also a hologram
and that every part of the body is a version
of the whole body would explain why
acupuncture, reflexology and homeopathy
work, and why every cell contains all the
information necessary to create an entire
human form.
This has tremendous implications. How can
reflexology and acupuncture find points
throughout the body that relates to
different organs may be explained by the
concept of holograms. The idea that placing
a needle at certain point in the foot, hand
or ear, affects different organs of the body
such as heart, liver or stomach makes sense
if one accepts the body as a hologram. Since
one of the properties of the hologram is
that every part of the body is a smaller
version of the whole, the whole body can be
found in the foot, hand or ear.
In the body hologram everything connects to
everything else and every cell is every
other cell. The concept of viewing the

universe as a hologram has been one of the most far reaching concepts of physics in modern times.

The theory that "reality," as we consciously experience it, is not real, goes back to indigenous people who believed that we exist in a dream or illusion. Theories about reality being a simulation are increasing, as well as the concept that the world we see is nothing but an illusion. Time is an illusion, the space-time continuum is an illusion, and so is everything else. The universe appears to be a consciousness hologram. Reality is a projected illusion within the hologram. Simulated reality is the hypothesis that reality could be simulated (for example by quantum computer simulation) to a degree indistinguishable from true reality. The holographic nature of the universe goes along with what Eastern philosophy and mystic literature teach, that the universe we live in is just an illusion of the senses, with no tangible reality.

Old physics, New Physics

For some 250 years we accepted the physics of Isaac Newton, the genius mathematician of the 17 century who published his most acclaimed work on physics in 1687. To him, time was seen as an arrow and atoms were the smallest parts of matter. He viewed the

world as a machine, and denied the existence
of the spirit because he thought he could
explain life without need for one.
Although his laws were successful to explain
gravity, the motion of planets and the
behavior of light, it failed miserably to
explain other physical phenomena which would
require an understanding of the functions of
the atom.
The universe was imagined to be a huge
clockwork in which six o'clock in New York
was six o'clock in Jupiter and in all stars.
Matter in the entire universe followed exact
physical rules on earth and nothing was left
to the imagination. Physicists were
comfortable believing they understood and
knew the physical world.
But this euphoria did not last very long.
All this changed with the coming of the
quantum theory. The quantum physics
demolished the long held "certainties" about
reality. In 1900, Mark Plank in Germany
proposed that energy was not continuous as
Newton thought, but occurred in small,
discrete packets called "quanta."
Then in 1905 Einstein postulated that light
consisted of these tiny quanta which were
later called photons, and that gained him
the Nobel Price. Today these photons are the
basis of TV, lasers, CT scans and most of
modern electronics.
In 1913 the brilliant Danish physicist Niels
Bohr gave science a major face lift with an

entirely new picture of the atom, one which resembles a miniature solar system with which we are all familiar. He described atoms as not being solid at all. They contain even smaller particles consisting of a nucleus (made of protons and neutrons) that appear to be circled by rotating electrons.

The atoms that comprise "physical matter" are overwhelmingly empty space. This empty space consists of energy vibrating on wavelengths that are higher than the physical, and even the particles were also found to be empty space as you go deeper in the subatomic realm.

He then discovered that the electrons did not behave in any way he had anticipated. Electrons were jumping orbits around the nucleus instantaneously, without traveling through the space between. This changed entirely our vision of the universe and how we see the physical matter.

The electrons move constantly. They not only vibrate or rotate in place, they also move through space, propelled by energy of the spin, not unlike a top, moving across the table as it spins.

By 1925 with the revolution quantum mechanics and the great contribution of well-known scientist, the theory of the atom was established and accepted by more and more physicists.

It was clear by then that atoms are not
solid at all, but are mostly 99.5 percent
space as Bohr had postulated.
According to recent research some 99.5
percent of all the mass in the universe is
lost to the five senses. We can only see
matter that reflects light and this is why
we cannot see in the dark. 99.5 of the mass
in the universe is called dark matter.
At this level, laws of conventional physics
do not seem to apply.
Things which appear to be solid to our
physical senses, such as walls, buildings,
mountains or bones, which we think are
solid, in reality have no solidity at all.
The particles move so fast that they appear
to be not here or there but everywhere at
once, thus creating the illusion of solidity
or physicality. Looking at the blades of a
fan in motion, or to the spokes of a bicycle
in motion, it produces the same effect; the
illusion of solidity. Since everything we
see and touch is made of atoms, scientist
became aware that the world we see is but an
illusion of the senses, a virtual reality
and nothing else. This is what the mystics,
Tibetan masters, Greek philosophers and
Eastern religions have been telling us for
centuries, that the world we see is Maya, or
illusion.
If you were to look at your body with
enormous magnification, what you will see is
exactly what you see when you look up at the

night sky. You will see that both are 99.5 percent space.

This similarity does not appear to be coincidence. As wise men of old told us "as above, so below"

A major change in how we see the physical world occurred when it was discovered that the mere act of observation played a role in the atomic world, something that was completely unsuspected by the physics model. The quantum physics theory is weird, bizarre, strange and difficult to understand, to say the least.

Subatomic particles were seen as waves when observed but when not under observation they behaved like particles. In the classic double slit experiment light was made to pass through two slits on a metal plate. Behind the plate was a screen. What they observed on the screen was that not only the particles had gone through both slits at the same time, but when they were observed, they became waves. In other words, the fact of observing the particles made them turn into waves. When the particles were observed, they behave as waves.

Thus, the observer effect not only changes the odds, it brings into existence the thing being observed. In essence, to observe a thing is to create the thing being observed.

To my knowledge, this was the first time that at laboratory level, it was shown that

consciousness creates the reality we see.
This confirms the shamans, and aboriginal
natives' views that we create our own
reality.

Chapter 3

The Mind Body Connection

Countless studies have shown that our thoughts affect the cells of the body and that they alter the pathways and the connections of the brain cells.
The human nervous system is the most complex of all systems with billions of neurons, multiple connections, electric impulses, chemical messengers and complex pathways in constant activity.
An example of this connection can be seen when we imagine cutting a lemon; our mouth begins to salivate. When a person is caught in a lie, or in an embarrassing situation the face will blush. This is because the small blood vessels of the face dilate, in an attempt to unconsciously cover the face. Sexual fantasies operate in a similar way. The sex organs respond as though a real sexual experience were taken place.

Water is particularly affected by our thoughts. This was demonstrated by the brilliant work of Japanese scientist Masaru Emoto, at the I.H.M. institute in Tokyo. He and his team exposed water to different thoughts and emotions, and then froze it to produce water crystals. When the crystals were observed under a microscope the response of the water was really amazing. The water that was exposed to loving thoughts and thoughts of appreciation, showed the most beautiful symmetrical an harmonious patterns, while the ones exposed to thoughts of hate and words like I hate you, I am going to kill you, showed ugly patterns of crystals in total disarray, completely asymmetrical, and without sequence. Since our body is about 70 percent water, is easy to see how thoughts can affect the body

"Every time you get angry, you poison your own system"

Alfred A. Montapert

In the XVII century Rene Descartes created a strict division between body and mind and this way of thinking has permeated the medical field for a long time to the extent that doctors considered the body a mechanical machine and nothing else. Today however it is known that stress debilitates the immune system, increases blood pressure and is thought to be responsible for the increased incidence of heart attacks.

The fact that thoughts affect the body can no longer be ignored.

The placebo effect is another good example of the effect the mind has over the body. A placebo is simply a medical treatment that has no effect at all on the body, but the patient believes he is receiving a powerful treatment.

In the medical field of research, no serious experiment has credibility unless the placebo effect is used in a double blind trial. One group of individuals are given a real treatment. The control group is given a fake treatment. Both groups think they are getting the real treatment. At the end of the experiment the result of both groups are compared. In such experiments neither the patients nor the researchers know what group is receiving the real treatment. Sugar pills are used as placebos, or saline injections which people usually think are more powerful than pills. It is estimated that at least forty percent of the people receiving a placebo will experience the anticipated effect, so, for a treatment to be effective it would have to show a response greater than the forty percent.

Surgery has also been used as a placebo, mainly in Europe. Patients were told that a surgical procedure would be necessary to remove the cause of their problem. The surgeon would just make an incision on the

skin and close it again without doing anything else, (sham surgery) leaving a surgical wound. Patients often reported miraculous cures. They frequently experienced just as much relief as the ones who had the full surgery.
In the fifties angina pectoris which is the pain produced by blockage of the coronary arteries of the heart, was treated with surgery, but it was later shown that this treatment had no effect whatsoever on the arteries of the heart, but many patients experienced immediate relief of their pain.

A case that illustrates the placebo effect was reported by a German physiologist Dr. Bruno Klopfer who was awarded a Ph.D. from the University of Munich in 1923 because of the profound impact he made in the development of psychological testing.
He treated a male patient for an advanced case of cancer in the lymph nodes. He had not responded to conventional treatment and had been given only a short time to live. He had developed large tumors in his neck, chest, groin and abdomen. Despite his poor prognosis he did not want to die.
He had heard of a new and exciting drug called Krebiozen, a substance obtained from blood of horses, initially said to be an effective treatment for cancer. In desperation and having nothing to lose, he begged his doctor to try the drug on him.

His doctor was reluctant to do it because he did not think it would work given the advanced stage of the disease, but at the insistence of the patient, he gave in and decided to let him try it.

His doctor was very surprised, when only a few days later, he found the patient out of bed and walking around. His tumors had shrunk to half of their original size. This was far more than any other treatment could have accomplished. The patient left the hospital ten days later feeling great, and cancer free.

The patient remained well for about two months, but then he read articles which began to appear asserting that the drug Krebiozen actually had no effect in cancer of the lymph nodes.

The patient became very depressed, suffered a relapse, tumors began to show again, and had to be re admitted to the hospital in poor condition.

This time his physician who knew about the placebo effect, decided to try an experiment. He told the patient that those reports were not accurate, that the drug was very effective but that the initial supplies of the drug had been damaged during shipping and rendered ineffective. He explained that he had a new concentration of the Krebiozen that was even more effective. His physician had no such drug but gave him a plain water injection which the patient was convinced it

was the powerful new medication.
This time again, the results were not short
of dramatic. The tumors which had recurred
disappeared; he experienced a complete and
rapid recovery and remained well until the
AMA (American Medical Association) announced
that the final study of the drug Krebiozen
had demonstrated that it was worthless in
the treatment of that type of cancer. This
time the patient's faith was completely
shattered, he entered a deep depression,
completely gave up, and died two days later.[2]

This was a very tragic case, but illustrates
how the mind bypassed his old beliefs and
tapped into the healing power within all of
us.
There are many similar cases of people
reporting miraculous cures caused by the
patient's belief and nothing else.
There are cases of patients who have lost
their hair believing they were taking
anticancer drugs.
These examples raise an important question;
what is in a placebo that creates such
unbelievable effect? Undoubtedly, their
belief affects the cells of the body in such
a way, as to create he expected action.

The placebo effect works in our daily lives.
Can you catch a cold by sitting in a draft?
Medical science has concluded that it does
not, yet people continue to catch colds in
these situations only because they believe

they do. People frequently take antibiotics for colds with good results, when we know that colds are caused by virus and antibiotics have no effect against virus. People believe that if they take coffee at night, it keeps them from going to sleep, yet experiments have shown that caffeine even injected in the veins has no such effect, unless they think it does. Another interesting question is: do drugs really work, or is it the placebo effect? The powerful pharmaceutical companies promote the notion that drugs heal people, but this is not the case, they remove symptoms at best.

While most doctors are aware of the placebo effect, few pay attention to the nocebo effect, which works similarly as the placebo effect but produces the opposite one, and can be as powerful as the placebo. If positive thinking can pull you out of depression, heal a broken bone, cure diseases considered incurable, think what negative suggestions can do to the body. They can severely damage the health of an individual. This negative effect is what is called the nocebo effect.
The belief that a treatment will not work, or that it will have harmful side effects, plays a significant role in the outcome of the treatment.

By the doctor's words and demeanor, they can

convey discouraging and negative messages to the patients. Statements such as: "you have an incurable disease", or "you only have three months to live", or "there is no cure for your disease", can have devastating effects. If the patient believes those statements to be true, the chances of cure are minimized.

The placebo effect unfortunately has not received in medical schools the attention it deserves and medical students continue to be taught the conventional treatments of drugs and surgery.
The placebo effect should be a major topic in their schools.
One of the reasons why the mind over body is not emphasized in medicine is not only do to our Newtonian way of thinking, but to the influence of the gigantic drug industry some of which are studying patients who respond to placebos for the purpose of eliminating them from their clinical trials. It is highly disturbing to their business to have patients that respond just as well to placebos as to the drugs. (Greenberg 2003,) Is it Prozac or placebo? M. Jones: 76-81)

The history of medicine is really the history of the placebo effect because doctors did not have the tools we have now to fight disease, and many cures were reported.
The topic of genetic diseases has been

gaining in popularity, to the point where some women who have perfectly normal breasts are having them removed because they have been told that they had a cancer gene and that it increases the chances of developing breast cancer.

I recently read about a well-known urologist who asked a surgeon to have his entire prostate removed because his father and two of his brothers had developed cancer of the prostate, and he thought he was carrying the prostate cancer gene. Fortunately, his surgeon talked him out of this way of thinking. These cases are just examples of the hysteria this genetic notion has created.

Dr. Bruce Lipton a former professor of medicine at Wisconsin University demonstrated at laboratory level that our beliefs affect all of the fifty trillion cells of our body and wrote a best seller book "The Biology of Belief," which has created the new way we look at biology and genetics.

We had been programmed by the biologist Central Dogma the belief that life is controlled by genes. He offered incontrovertible evidence to prove that biology most cherished teachings regarding genetic were fundamentally flowed.

He discovered that cell life is controlled by the physical and energetic environment,

45

with only small contribution by the genes. He explains that genes are just genetic blueprints used in the construction of cells, tissues and organs. The belief that we are frail, biochemical machines controlled by genes is giving way to the understanding that we are powerful creators of our lives and the world in which we live.

Scientists have made lots of links to many diseases but they have rarely found that one gene causes a trait or a disease.
In human disease, defective genes acting alone only account for no more than two percent of the disease load.
Dr. Lipton writes that the notion of genes controlling biology has been repeated for so long that scientists have forgotten it was just a hypothesis, not truth and that it was never proved.
He, courageously, facing great opposition from his peers, who were stuck in old dogmas and beliefs, that mind does not count in biology, published his new biology, which has in turn created the new science of epigenetics, which means control above genetics. It has established that DNA blueprints passed down through genes are not set at birth, so, that genes are not destiny.3
He was exhilarated by the realization that he could change the character of his life by changing his beliefs.

One more interesting aspect of the body mind connection is that of the Multiple Personality Disorder also known as Dissociative Identity Disorder. It is a condition wherein a person's identity is fragmented into two or more distinct personality states. This is frequently the result of severe abuse. In addition to possessing different brain-wave patterns, these personalities have a strong psychological separation from one another. In one personality a subject may have warts in his hands, which are not present when another personality comes in. A person may be diabetic and yet when another personality is manifested there is no trace of the disease. Allergies have also been noticed in one personality, but not in the other. In one report, a patient had severe allergic reaction to a wasp sting in one of the eyes. This reaction completely cleared when an alternate personality became manifested, but the painful condition along with the severe eye swelling returned when the original personality with the allergic reaction took control of the body.

By changing personalities, a multiple that is drunk can become instantly sober in another personality. A patient wearing glasses in one personality may have perfect vision in another. It has also been found that the voice pattern for each of the

personalities is different, which is quite a remarkable change.
Tumors have also been noted to disappear and reappear with change of personality.
Even the color of the eyes have been noticed to change when an alternate was manifested. These incredible mind-boggling changes that take place with the mere change of personality, remain a mystery but is a clear indication of the mind-body connection. Obviously, what we think and believe affects how the body responds.

I know about the case of Richard Alpert, a former psychologist at Harvard University who later became a mystic and changed his name to Ram-Dass. He was investigating the effects of LSD and as part of his research he traveled in the 60's to the Himalayas where he met a holy man. This holy man asked him to give him a large dose of LSD, and then a lethal dose, but the drug had no effect whatsoever on him, because he knew the LSD was an illusion. This holy man had a firm belief that nothing from the outside could have an effect on his body, even a lethal dose of a chemical. On the other side of the coin, there are reports of people having taken a placebo, believing it was LSD, who experienced all the effects of the drug.

The phenomenon of the mysterious stigmata where people bleed through wounds in their hands and feet just like Jesus did on the cross, is a potent expression of the power the mind has over the body. In the old days Christianity looked at these cases as representing spirituality, but the phenomenon has been experienced by many fanatics whose minds are so focused on the wounds of Jesus that they produce similar if not identical wounds.

These people have seen paintings and images of Jesus on the cross with holes in his hands and feet, but it was the custom of the Romans at the time, to bang the nails through the wrists of those they crucified because they knew the hands were not able to support the weight of the body.

People who have produced the stigmata believed that the wounds were in the hands and it is where they developed them.

These are signs of the power of their belief, and the wounds are produced by their minds. Some researchers believe that the stigmata are the effect of PK, or psychokinesis, which is the ability to affect objects with the force of thought alone. Bohm believes that the body, not being separated from the mind, responds to beliefs and convictions, and that thoughts create a response in the body, which explains the appearance of the wounds and bleeding typical of stigmata.

There are many cases of stigmata, and

perhaps one of the best well known is that of a German nun, Therese Neumann. Her wounds bled profusely and this was witnessed by many U.S. servicemen stationed in Germany after the war. They visited her because of her miraculous abilities. But one of the most remarkable feats of this unusual nun was her ability to produce *inedia,* the supernormal ability to live without food. She subsisted solely on liquids for many years. She then gave up drinking liquids, so she was not receiving any food or water at all. She had a strong conviction that she could survive on the energy of the air alone. She believed that God was in the air and that it was all she needed. Many reporters flooded to her, but eventually they disappeared as they became frustrated with not being able to create any more news or explain her strange ability.

When the local bishop learned about Neumann's claims, he sent a commission to investigate her. She was under constant supervision, and Franciscan nurse sisters monitored her every move. Many tests were done including stool analysis which confirmed that there was no evidence of any food residue at all. Curiously, she never showed any signs of dehydration, and her weight remained constant. It appears that she was not only materializing the significant amounts of blood necessary to replace the blood loss though her stigmata,

but also the necessary nutrients she needed to stay alive and in good health. There are many other cases through religious literature of Madonna's shedding tears, and many cases of head wounds resembling Jesus' caused by the crown of thorns.
These unexplained occurrences baffle researchers, unable to come up with an explanation.

Experiments with Israeli soldiers and others have shown that they did not get tired because of how far they have walked so much as how much they thought they have walked. Blood test found that the stress hormone levels in the soldier's blood always reflected what they thought they had walked and not the actual distance they had marched. Their bodies responded not to the real distance but what they believed was real because the human body cannot differentiate between a real experience and what we believe the experience is.

Another example of mind over body is the case of fire walking. Fire walking is the act of walking barefoot over a bed of hot embers or coals. It has been practiced by many people and cultures in many parts of the world.
In 2005 a woman by the name of Amanda Dennison, of Alberta, Canada was registered in the Guinness Book of Records for the longest documented fire walk ever. Although

many people have done this type of walking
without any injury at all, what made
Amanda's case different was that she walked
220 feet through a bed of glowing coals at
1,700 degrees Fahrenheit, without any injury
at all.
These experiences teach a profound lesson
about the power of the mind, and the effect
that our thoughts and beliefs have on how we
experience reality.

There are many reports of people who under
certain circumstances have lifted a car to
free a person pinned under it. One of these
stories was aired by the BBC News on August
4th, 2005 of a woman who lifted over 20 times
her body weight to free a friend who was
trapped under her car after an accident,
even though she herself was injured. "I just
knew I had to set him free," she said.
If these cases happen to some people, it is
an indicative that we all possess a
"something" available to all of us.
These cases pose a question: how are these
case possible? It appears that we live our
lives based on what we believe is possible
and what is impossible. Under certain
conditions our minds rewrite the program,
our belief system is bypassed in favor of
another belief that says: yes you can.
The power of the belief system affecting not
only the body, but our environment is real,
and cannot longer be ignored.

One possible explanation for these miracles is the holographic model. The hot coals are a hologram, and so are the feet, they are both illusions, so, how can one illusion affect another? Only because we think it does, so, if we change the program, we can walk on the hot coals with no pain and no injury at all.

   "If you think you can or that you cannot you are right"

Henry Ford

Chapter 4

Meditation

A few years ago, certainly in the West,
meditations was spoken of in a whisper, and
any one known to teach or practice this art
was looked upon as odd, as weird or "not
quite there."
Our society had been functioning so purely
in the physical that meditation had not
received any attention. This attitude has
changed over the years and today there are
millions of people who have taken this art
as part of their lives.
Meditation can be defined as a self-induced
specific state of consciousness where the
mind and body are at rest and the attention
is focused on the breath and relaxation of
the body to achieve an emotional calm state.
It can also transform the mind from a
disturbed condition to a peaceful one.

Meditation is an art and like all arts, it
has to be practiced daily, not taken up for
a few days and laid aside. It is persistent
perseverance that will achieve the goal.
First, there is a retreat from the senses,
no emotional pressure, absolute relaxing of

the body, but the mind is awakened and alive to spiritual impressions.

Meditation is about touching the source essence, which is in all of us. It is about getting into a space where you are no longer concerned with the noisy physical world and mundane thoughts, and start becoming aware that there is a You, who is watching you. You become aware that you are more than your physical body.

The ancient methods of meditation were all developed in the East. The Eastern mind is very patient from thousands of years of teaching to remain patient, whatever the condition may be. The Western mind is very impatient, and this is why the great spiritual teacher Osho, one of the most provocative and inspiring spiritual teachers of the twentieth century says that the same methods of technique cannot be applied to both.[4]

He also says that meditation "Is the switch that can silence the mind. A sharper, more relaxed and creative mind, one that can function at the peak of its intelligence."

Meditation can transform a state of confusion into a state of clarity. The mind is in constant chattering, and that is the main obstacle we encounter when we try to meditate; thoughts create clouds, and the clarity is lost. When thoughts disappear, is when clarity happens.

It has been said that you can have either mind or meditation, but not both, because mind is thinking and meditation is silence, so, they cannot coexist.

Meditation itself requires no technique at all; it is a simple understanding, an alertness, an awareness. But on the way to being alert, there are many obstacles, and the function of all techniques of meditation is to prepare the ground, to prepare the way by quieting the constant activity of mind. Osho tells us that meditation is something natural, something that is hidden inside you and is trying to reach to the open sky and to the sun. But the mind being the main obstacle, closes all doors and windows. The techniques are needed to open the windows and doors, and immediately the whole sky is available to you, with all the stars, with all its beauty, with all the sunsets and sunrises. Just as a small grain of sand can go into your eye and prevent you from seeing the vast sky because you cannot open your eyes. It seems illogical that a small grain of sand can prevent you from seeing the great stars and the infinite sky. But in fact it can, and techniques are needed to remove that grain of sand from your eyes. In the same way, techniques serve only to quiet the mind thus removing the obstacle.

There are many types of meditation, and innumerable books have been written on this subject, dealing mainly with the different techniques and philosophies behind them.

This chapter is not intended to give an in-depth study on the subject but to give the reader basic information on what meditation is. I will just mention the types of meditation that I have experienced firsthand Transcendental Meditation or TM as it is known, was created by Maharishi Mahesh Yogi. This form of meditation became very popular in the 60's as many people and celebrities such as the Beatles were instructed in the technique.

In this type of meditation the student is given a specific key word also known as "mantra" which is unique to each student, and is to be repeated over and over again with eyes closed and with relaxed body and a relaxed mental state, for about twenty minutes every day.

Dr. Benson, professor of medicine at Harvard, created a variation of this technique, where instead of using a given personal word as mantra, the students were instructed to simply repeat the word "one," over and over again for the same twenty minutes a day.

The results were analyzed a few months later and were found to be remarkably positive.

The benefits of meditation have been confirmed in many different studies. These benefits include drop in blood pressure,

improved memory, increases ability to
concentrate, increased ability to control
anxiety, improved sleep patterns,
improvement in heart rate, and balance of
the brain hemispheres, to mention but a few.
Meditation has also been proven to boost
many of the body's chemicals such as GABA,
endorphins, and others, while lowering
stress hormones such as cortisol.
In general, there was an improvement in
physical and mental health.
The EOC Institute lists 141 benefits of mind
body and emotions from meditation.
A group of 7,000 people meditating on
thoughts of love, peace, and happiness were
able to reduce acts of terrorism worldwide
by 72 percent. The level of crimes and
fatalities all dropped remarkably just from
this small group of people meditating
privately. This study was documented in a
scientific study published in the "Journal
of Offender Rehabilitation"

Another form of meditation is the one
devised by Jose Silva, author of the Silva
Mind Control. Mr. Silva did extensive
research mainly with children, who are
naturally psychic. His method of meditation
is geared more towards problem solving and
to create conditioning for success.
In this technique, students are instructed
to close their eyes, take a deep breath and
while exhaling to mentally visualize the

number three, three times, with another
breath the number two three times and then
the number one three times, while making
suggestions of complete physical and mental
relaxation. At this level, the brain waves
which in the normal wake state are around
twenty per second (beta waves) dropped to
around ten per second (alpha waves). With
alpha waves, the mind is more susceptible to
receive suggestions. He then proceeded to
make suggestions regarding their good
health, increased learning abilities,
increased concentration and any other
suggestions to create the desired effects on
the students. He would then program them
with triggers like bringing thumb, index and
middle fingers together to reactivate the
alpha state. Every time they used the
trigger, it would immediately re-create the
alpha state, and increase their ability to
perform during activities throughout the
day. The students were able to program
weight loss, ability to relax, improvement
in their sleep patterns, create instant
relaxation and other desired conditions. I
witnessed several people successfully
programmed to lose weight without going into
a diet, just by developing the mental image
of the physical shape they wanted to have.

The technique is similar to hypnosis with
the difference that unlike hypnosis in which
you are not conscious and depend entirely on

the hypnotist, in this method you are always in control, you can accept or reject anything that is suggested to you, and you are fully conscious and awake.

Kriya yoga is a different type of meditation. It was brought to the United States from India by the founder of the Self Realization Fellowship, Paramahansa Yogananda. It was created by the Great Babaji who lives in the Himalayan Mountains. This great mystic is hundreds of years old but appears to be no older than twenty five. He has a strong body, dark lustrous eyes and long hair, and requires no food. He can materialize and dematerialize his deathless body anytime, anywhere and take any physical form at will. He lives a few miles south of the Tibetan border.
Although Kriya yoga has the same physical benefits of other types of meditation, the main purpose of it is to reach what is known as Self Realization. This is a state of consciousness where you realize that the real You, (and not your physical form) is one with Cause (all there is, source, or God). In part of this meditation, you dis-identify with who you appear to be. You are not your body, you are not your thoughts, you are not your mental hang ups, your nationality, your gender, your profession, nor your name or your titles. So, who are you? Then the answer comes; you are pure

consciousness, all pure spirit. Just as a drop of water falls into the ocean and becomes the ocean, your individual consciousness merges with the universal consciousness and becomes one with it.
On another part of this meditation, you are led to feel the presence of God in every cell, in every atom of your being.
This is a powerful kind of meditation for those who want spiritual development besides the physical benefits.

Another entirely different type of meditation was developed by Joel Goldsmith (1892-1964) author of "The Infinite Way," and several other books. He was an American businessman who after having a spiritual experience became one of the most inspiring and provocative spiritual teachers or modern times. Once he realized that meditation was the way, he meditated only for two or three minutes at a time but no less than twenty times a day. He would go into relaxation and try to "listen" to the voice of his higher Self. It took him about nine months before he started having any impressions. These vague impressions became clearer and clearer, to the point where he was getting complete messages. This form of meditation emphasizes making an effort to be aware of the presence of God at all times, under any circumstances.[5]
He was then lead to develop The Infinite

Way, and then started to lecture all over the world.

The Infinite way, is a spiritual teaching consisting of principles which anyone may follow and practice, irrespective of his religious affiliation. The purpose of the infinite way meditation as in the case of Kriya yoga is to reach a state in which we become aware of the constant presence of God in our consciousness, and the realization that God and us are one, which is known as self-realization.

His inspiring lectures are still available through the Infinite Way headquarters in Moreno Valley, CA.

Whenever he lectured, the topic was never announced because he never knew it in advance. The whole lecture would be dictated to him by a "voice" in his head and he only knew what he had said after he listened to the recorded lectures.

He wrote many books, and often spoke about how much he had learned from them. As in lecturing, in writing books he would be told what to write.

The type of meditation he practiced was his own, and different from the recommended fifteen to twenty minutes a day.

The case of Goldsmith is a good indication that meditation does not have to follow any particular pattern, as it is a personal experience.

The bottom line of meditation, regardless of techniques and methods, is to connect with the God within. To recognize that we are much more than our physical and mental self, and realize that we are universal consciousness, one with all it is, all powerful, with no limitations except for the ones we accept as real.

Chapter 5

Imagination

"Imagination is more important than knowledge because knowledge is limited while imagination has no bounds"

Albert Einstein

Imagination, or creative visualization is the technique of using visual mental images to create what you want in life. It is not difficult to form a mental picture. Everyone does so to a greater or lesser extent, and day dreams are such pictures.
There is really nothing unusual about it. You use it all the time whether you are aware if it or not.
Everything you see: cars, houses, buildings, were at one time only in the imagination of the builder. Where did these objects come from? Only from one source: the amazing power of imagination

"Consciousness is always the seed and the Cause behind all physical manifestation. Any physical appearance is merely the Effect. Everything begins with

consciousness, in the realm of the immaterial"

Cabbalist Rav Berg

The word imagination has been used to indicate all types of ideas, some of them contradictory. We ask someone to use his imagination, meaning that his present outlook seems ineffective to do a task. At other times, we may say that his ideas are pure imagination, meaning that they do not make much sense. We may also refer to a jealous or suspicious person as victim of his own imagination, meaning that his suspicions are not true.
On the other hand, we may refer to someone as a person of great imagination, meaning that he is successful in carrying out his own ideas. In this chapter we refer to imagination as creative visualization.

The man who uses his imagination successfully knows that it is the inner world of imagination that is the real cause of the visible outside world. Every man should be conscious of the fact that the inner causal world of imagination is the source of the outer world of effects.

Consider the following quote:

"Imagination is the very gateway to

Reality"

William Blake

The moment man discovers that imagination is the gateway to reality he can accomplish acts which can only be called miraculous. He has the power to be and have anything he desires. When we understand the force of imagination, we hold in our hands the key to the solution of our problems.

Nikola Tesla, perhaps the most renowned inventor of the last century, relied heavily on his great capacity to visualize. He learned the secret of visualization at an early age, encouraged by his mother. In his autobiography, he describes how he always visualized each invention to the most minimal detail. He wrote that more important than any laboratory is the development of the imagination. He worked out all of his inventions in his mind. In his imagination he would test them, correct any defects and then visualize the end product, before he took his ideas to the laboratory.

There have been many studies from the Soviets regarding the use of imagery as treatment for many conditions. They have also incorporated sophisticated imagery techniques in many of their athletic programs, and they believe that the mental images affect the neuromuscular system in a similar way as the athletes who do the actual physical work.

In a study reported by Charles A. Garfield author of "Peak Performance, the Mental Training Techniques of The world's Greatest Athletes" and former researcher of NASA, a group of the world-class Soviet athletes was divided into four groups. The first group spent 100 percent of their training time in actual physical training.
The second spent 75 percent of their time in physical training and 25 percent of their time visualizing the exact movements and accomplishments they wanted to achieve in their sport. The third group spent 50 percent of their time in physical training and 50 percent visualizing and the fourth spent 25 percent in physical training and 75 percent visualizing. Although is appears hard to believe, at the 1980 Winter Games in Lake Placid, New York, the fourth group, which spent most of the time visualizing showed the greatest improvement in performance, followed by groups three, two and one, in that order![6]

Similar results were mentioned by Michael Talbot in his book The Holographic Universe. Australian psychologist Alan Richardson took three groups of basketball players and tested their ability to make free throws. Then he instructed the first group to spend twenty minutes a day practicing free throws. He told the second group not to practice at all, and had the third group spend twenty minutes a day visualizing that they were shooting perfect baskets. As expected the group that did nothing had no improvement. The first group improved 24 percent, but the third group, using the power of imagination alone improved an astonishing 23 percent, almost as much as the group who did the actual free throws.

The Soviets are known to have done many similar studies. In one of them, a group of elderly men in a nursing home were selected. One group was instructed to lift weights for twenty minutes every day. The second group received instructions to relax in a comfortable position and vividly imagine that they were lifting the same size weights as the first group, and to practice this technique for the same amount of time every day. After three months, the muscular development of the group practicing visualization showed slightly more muscular mass than the group actually lifting the weighs.

The fact that visualization accomplishes great results is something that I have confirmed myself time and time again. The early stages of my visualization were mentioned in the first chapter of this book.

"Man becomes what he imagines"

Neville

Does a firm persuasion that a thing is, will make it so? And the prophet replied "All poets believe that it does, and in ages of imagination, the firm persuasion removed mountains, but many are not capable of firm persuasion"

William Bake in "Knowledge of Heaven

And Hell."

In the Best Selling classic "The Power of Awareness" researcher and writer Neville Goddard lists case after case of people succeeding in making their dreams a reality using the power of imagination. He has also written other books on this subject and has great experience teaching his students how to fulfill their desires using mental pictures and assuming the attitude of the wish fulfilled.

Imagination, he says, is the instrument by which you create your world.

When man develops the power of imagination, he will have discovered the secret of causation, and that is: Imagination creates reality. Therefore, the man who is aware of what he is imagining knows that he is creating; he realizes more and more that creation is imagination first, then it becomes physical. Men possess the power to create reality, but this power sleeps as though dead, when not consciously exercised. The future must become the present in the imagination of the one who would wisely and consciously create circumstances.

Neville states also that when imagination is not controlled and the attention not focused on the feeling of the wish fulfilled, then no amount of prayer, piety or invocation will produce the desired effect. When you can call up at will whatsoever you please, when the forms of your imagination are as vivid as the forms of nature, you are master of your fate.[7]

The twelfth-century Persian Sufis concluded that imagination is the faculty of perception and they gave it the greatest importance.

They believed that one can use visualization to alter and reshape one's aspirations and destiny.

Objective reality, writes Fichte, is "solely produced through imagination". Objects seem so independent of our perception of them, that we are inclined to forget that they owe their reality to imagination. The world in which we live is a world of imagination and man through his imagination creates the realities and circumstances of life.

The attempt to change circumstances before you change your imagination is to struggle against the very nature of things. There can be no outer change until there is first an imagination change.

Most writers on the power of imagination agree that for imagination to be most effective one needs to create the feeling of the wish fulfilled. That is, we need to see what we desire as already happening. We need to be able to see it in our mind, touch it, interact with it and consider it as real.

The power of imagination appears to work in the physical body, because it has been established by researchers that the human nervous system cannot tell the difference between a real experience and one that is vividly imagined. The cells of the body react exactly in the same manner.

When you imagine eating a lemon, your mouth begins to salivate, because to the salivary cells you are in fact eating a lemon, they respond in the same way, and this goes for all the rest of the cells of the body.

"Man is all imagination. God is man and exists in us and us in Him. The eternal Body of man is the imagination, that is, God Himself"

Blake

This has tremendous implications, and one wonders what our society would be like if we taught our children the technique of visualization beginning in the early school years.

Chapter 6

Hypnosis

Hypnosis can be defined as a state of consciousness involving much focused attention, and reduced peripheral awareness where the conscious mind is set aside, so that the subconscious mind is open to respond to any suggestions. It has been verified as an effective technique that can promote human change. To this effect, it has been used in pain management, goal setting, stress reduction, in managing sleep disorders, weight loss programs, anger management, enhance the ability of public speaking, and other desirable conditions.

Hypnosis has been used also as a form of entertainment to amuse audiences, and this is an aspect of hypnosis with which most people are familiar.
Hypnosis is also called mesmerism, because of Franz Anton Mesmer's early contribution to development of this art. Mesmer was a German physician interested in animal magnetism. In the year 1843 the Scottish physician James Braid proposed the term

hypnosis.

To better understand what hypnosis is, it is very important to know the difference between the conscious and the subconscious mind.

The conscious mind is the part of the mind we use while engaged in our normal daily activities, it is the seat of our personal identity, the creative mind we use to plan our future, review the past and use logical thought in problem solving and in daily social interactions.

The subconscious mind on the other hand, plays a different role than our conscious mind. It is much larger and more powerful than the conscious one. It is estimated that the subconscious is responsible for about 95 percent of the activity of our daily lives although we are usually not aware of it and we may be completely oblivious to the fact that it exists at all. It is the part of the mind that is responsible for automatic body functions. It makes our hearts beat, our lungs breath, and is responsible for many other biological functions like digestion, assimilation and elimination. It works instinctively, without our conscious mind intervening. It never sleeps, and it comes to our assistance in case of life threatening situations, since its main function is to keep us alive. In any situation that require a split-second decision it is the subconscious mind that makes the decisions because it is much faster than its conscious counterpart.

According to cell biologist Bruce Lipton, Ph.D., the conscious mind operates with the computer processing power of 40 bits of information per second, while the subconscious processes it at 20 million bits per second. This means that the subconscious is 500,000 bits faster.

The truth is that most people enter a trance state on a daily basis, like when you lose track of time when driving long distances, watching TV, or exposed to a repetitive monotonous sound. In a typical hypnosis session, the hypnotist, after inducing a trance like state, makes suggestions according to the desired result. The subconscious mind obeys the suggestions without any interference from the conscious. The hypnotist, once he or she will have you relaxed into a trance like state that allows powerful access to the subconscious mind, will then implant the messages they want you to follow.

Michael Talbot Ph.D. in his book "The Holographic Universe" mentions a case he witnessed where a hypnotist was hired to entertain guests at a party. He hypnotized a man called Tom and told him than when he returned to his normal waking state he would not be able to see his daughter. Before he clicked his fingers to break the trance, he led the daughter to stand right in front of her father, so Tom was sitting down right in front of her.

When Tom came out of the trance state, he was asked if he would see his daughter in the room. "No," he said. His daughter started laughing but Tom could not hear her. The hypnotist went then behind the daughter and put his hand behind her lower back. He said he was holding something in his hand and asked Tom what it was. Tom was a little bemused because it seemed so obvious to him. "You are holding a watch," he said. The hypnotist asked if he could read the inscription on the watch and Tom did so. All the time his daughter was standing between him and the watch.8

This appears fantastic, or impossible. How could he see the watch behind her and not see her? Because the hypnotist had implanted the belief that his daughter was not there, and his subconscious mind constructed the new reality that she was not to be seen. Since his daughter was not seen, there was nothing to keep Tom from seen the watch behind her.

This case shows how the subconscious mind goes to work according to the suggestions given, without any interference from the conscious mind.

Hypnotists who give shows for entertainment purpose frequently make the hypnotized

person perform ridiculous acts, he may say
something like "after you wake up, when I
snap my fingers you will bark like a dog,"
and the subject will just do that, to the
amusement of the audience. As stated before,
the conscious mind of a person under
hypnosis cannot interfere.

It is remarkable how conditions of the body
can be changed under hypnotic suggestion.
Even congenital conditions, which means
altering the master plan of our DNA
programming itself. One such case took place
where a sixteen year old boy afflicted by a
terrible disfiguring hereditary genetic
condition called Brocq's disease was cured
by a hypnotist named A.A. Mason at the Queen
Victoria Hospital in East Grinstein,
England. Patients afflicted with this
disease develop a thick, horn like layer
covering over their skin that resembles the
scales of reptiles. The skin becomes
hardened and rigid so that even the
slightest movement can cause the skin to
tear, crack, produce severe pain and bleed.
This disease had never been cured before
1951 where this incident took place. The
hypnotist made the suggestion to the boy,
under hypnosis, that his condition was
clearing and that soon would be gone. Just
five days later the heavy scaly layer
covering the boy's left arm fell off,
exposing healthy, soft skin. By the end of

the ten days the arm was completely normal, and eventually the boy was completely cured and remained symptom free for at least five years at which point Mason lost touch with the boy. This amazing success was reported in the British Medical Journal.9

There are many other reports of the so called incurable diseases which have been cured with hypnosis, which basically means convincing the subconscious mind that the body is healthy, and this unconscious belief is what accounts for the incredible healings.
Several studies have shown that until the age of seven, our brains are extremely receptive to any suggestions, they are in what is called hypnagogic or dreamlike state, and in this condition they absorb like sponges and record any information and any sound around them. Everything they see and any emotion felt, is recorded without any filter to tell them what is true and what is false. Their brains even record sounds and impressions before birth, such as discussions between parents, mother's emotions and everything around them.

The Jesuits know this very well and this is why it's founder, Ignatius of Loyola said: "Give me a child until he is seven, and I will give you the man."
The religious beliefs instilled in their minds as young children would stay with them

through their adult lives.

The subconscious mind is primarily
repository of stimulus-response tapes
created by previous experiences. It is
habitual and will play automatically the
same tape in response to life situations
over and over again, much to our chagrin.
This is the reason we keep making the same
mistakes over and over again.
We think we are running our lives with our
decisions and wishes created consciously,
but the true is that it is not the case, we
tend to act according to our deep programmed
beliefs as neuroscience has shown us.
It has also shown us that the conscious mind
runs the show only about 5 percent of the
time at best. The programmed subconscious
shape 95 percent of our life experience.
If the desires of the conscious mind
conflict with the tapes recorded in
childhood, the subconscious mind always
wins.
If as a child you were exposed to comments
like you are worthless, or you are not
capable, or to phrases like you will never
amount to anything, etc., these messages
programmed in the subconscious will
undermine any conscious efforts to succeed
in our work and life in general. This
accounts for the failure of our good
intentions at work, in business and in our
relationships. This, to some extent is also

responsible for the failure of the New Year's resolutions.

The subconscious mind has no sense of humor, has no flexibility, and takes everything presented to it as a fact, weather it is true or false. The program begins in infancy. We hear that uncle Joe lost his job, mother became sick, father broke a leg and was rushed to the hospital, we cannot afford, there is never enough, this child is always sick, and a litany of other negative suggestions which the subconscious absorbs without questioning its validity. The result is that by age seven, we are well negatively programmed for life! We have accepted as real and valid the concepts of scarcity, illness and a host of other negative programs.

There is another interesting aspect of subconscious programming, called subliminal programming.

This type of programming is carried out by key words or images of which we are not consciously aware. Phrases such as "buy this car," or, "you need to drink this." It could be an image, or a picture, placed in such way that is not obvious to the conscious mind, but the subconscious mind does not miss a thing and absorbs all of it. This is used very cleverly in advertisement. The brain receives the images through the eyes or ears and decodes into conscious thoughts

and language; like I want that car, or I need this drug. TV shows and movies are packed with hidden messages and children are particularly vulnerable. They are being brainwashed by subliminal messages to turn into insatiable consumers.
Some clever politicians use this system to win votes, while we are not aware in the least that we are being programmed.
We have seen an increase in obesity, and diabetes and our dependency on drugs has increased in unprecedented numbers, to a certain degree, due to TV subliminal programming.

Is it not possible that the human race is in a hypnotic trance every bit as real as Tom's; even more so? In the story, Tom had only the hypnotist working on him and for a short time. In everyday life we are constantly bombarded with hypnotic suggestions from the media, from the government, from advertisers, from our peers and from many other sources.
When we are young we are told by parents what is real and what is not, what is acceptable or possible, and what is not. Then we go to school and teachers will continue our "indoctrination." We live our entire lives being programmed by others, and we construct our reality to fit the program. No wonder why we have completely forgotten who and what we really are. We have

forgotten that we can do anything we want to do, that we are all powerful souls occupying a body temporarily. God created us in his image and likeness, but we have returned the compliment and have created a God in our image and likeness; a vengeful God, capable of human emotions, just waiting for us to die, to judge us. A deaf God who does not listen to our prayers, far away somewhere, unreachable and aloof.

What a sad picture of God we have been programmed to believe. I am not surprised there are many atheists.

When you plant a seed in the ground, "something" makes it grow into a plant. When we eat, that food turns by a magic something into hair, nails, muscles, skin, and every other part of our bodies. That is the same something that makes the atoms vibrate and planets rotate around the sun. That "something" is considered by some eastern philosophies to be God. When Atheists consider what that something is and what it does, will then believe that that "something" does in fact exist.

The truth is that we are all Gods, and this knowledge is what is understood by Self Realization. Jesus was a man not unlike any of us, with one great difference; he knew he was God, we still do not know that.

Going back to the issue of being negatively programmed, many times in my career I had

the opportunity to see patients who were
healthy, and yet would make comments such as
well… after all, I am over forty or, what do
you expect? I am over forty, meaning that
they had passed the point at which they
begin to experience all sorts of age related
physical problems.
This of course is nonsense. There is
absolutely no reason at all for the common
belief that as we age everything will begin
to malfunction. We create a new body every
seven years, so, in reality the oldest our
bodies are is seven years, but as long as we
believe that getting old is getting sick, it
will be so for us.

It appears as though the universe only knows
the word yes. It is like a gigantic Xerox
machine. If we feel we are poor, the
universe says: yes, you are. Is this not the
reason certain prayers do not work? Every
time we say give me, or I need, what we are
actually saying is: I don't have it, and the
universe responds in the affirmative. Give
us the daily bread means we don't have it,
and the answer is, yes, you don't have it.
True prayer is not an act of asking, but an
act of thankfulness. "Even before you ask,
it is given to you."

Another interesting aspect of how the
subconscious mind can be programmed is what
takes place in Mind Control Programs. Secret
government programs started in US in the

twenties and have continued to this date. Other countries have similar programs. An individual's subconscious mind is programmed to forget his past which is replaced by a new one; his personality is entirely changed to be used for sinister purposes. I would not elaborate on these programs but the reader can find excellent information with actual videos, interviews of survivors and photographs, on U tube looking for the Montauk project, carried out on military bases at Montauk, NY, among many other mind control programs.

Chapter 7

Channeling

Channeling is a way of communication between humans and nonhuman beings. A channel can be compared to a language translator or interpreter. The channel will translate the communication into human language.

Some people may fear this process because they don't understand it and are afraid that some dark uninvited entity can enter without their permission. This is not the case. Channelers are generally highly evolved beings who may or may not have had a physical existence but no longer focused on physical matter, choose carefully the channel according to the message to be delivered and the degree of preparation and character of the channel.
Although channeling has been recorded throughout history, and many books have been written on this subject, it has received more attention during the last thirty years, and today one can find hundreds of available channeling books and videos, as the subject has become more popular.
We need to be aware that not all channelers

are getting information from other
dimensions but from their own psyche. There
are many entities from other realms that use
channels to manipulate and mislead, so we
need to be very selective and investigate
what the message says before we give it our
attention.

Channelers, not having a physical body,
cannot speak in any human language, so, they
use all of the channel's physical and mental
abilities to convey the message.

The channeler transmits the telepathic
message and the channel's brain decodes it
into words.

In most cases the channel goes into an
altered state of consciousness or trance,
but this is not always the case.

Sometimes the nonhuman entity transmits the
message to the channel in full awake state
of consciousness in what is called automatic
writing. In this method of communication,
the channel writes down the message in full
consciousness, but having no input or
control into what is being written. In other
cases, the channel fully awaken, and with
full control, simply takes note of what is
being dictated and this is how "A Course in
Miracles" was produced.

There are many inspiring and full of wisdom
channeling occurrences which give us
knowledge on several subjects which are
otherwise not available to us. There are
many channeling reports, but I will mention

only the few that I know to be legitimate and had the opportunity to study. I have found them to be of great benefit to me personally.

Since this is such an unusual way to communicate, people have the tendency to get hung up on the identity of the messenger and not focusing in the message, wonder if it is all fake and begin to doubt its validity. My recommendation would be: if the message is helpful, if it makes sense to you, if it gives information on how to solve your problems, if you feel uplifted by it, that is what is important.

The very first book I ever read on this subject in the early seventies was "Seth Speaks," channeled by Jane Roberts.

It is a practical guide to conscious living. It articulates the great reaches of human potential and presents an alternate map of reality, useful to all explorers of consciousness.

It teaches that each individual has access to intuitional knowledge and can get glimpses of inner reality. As other similar sources, it states that it is consciousness that creates reality, and not the other way around. It teaches that our physical reality is a perfect replica of our inner thoughts and feelings, and that the characteristic of materializing thoughts and emotions into physical reality is an attribute of the soul.

It states that not all personalities are physical, and that we do not realize that there is a portion of us whose own powers are far superior to those shown by our ordinary self. The book emphasizes that all of us have lived other existences and that knowledge is within us though we are not consciously aware of them. It teaches that no reality exists but that which is created by consciousness. We are so fascinated with physical reality, that we are in as deep a trance now as when we are asleep. There are many other realities, but we ignore their existence and blot out all stimuli coming from them. We don't seem to realize that we are creating our body at each moment as a direct result of our inner conception of what we are, and that our physical reality is created in perfect replica of our inner desires, thoughts and feelings. The book further teaches that we possess the magic power of transforming thoughts and emotions into physical counterparts.10

Lazaris is another channeler who gives information through Jack Purcel. The Lazaris material is a spark of love. In that spark of love, there is healing, laughter, growth through joy and much more. The emphasis of his messages as is the case of other channelers is that we create our own reality, and goes into detail as to what reality is and how we create it all. This channeler has helped thousands of individuals to reorient their lives, and solve their problems in ways not presented to them before.

One of the most popular channelers of recent times is "Abraham" channeled by Esther Hicks. This entity gives advice on very practical issues such as how to create more abundance in our lives, how to create wealth and how to solve many our day to day problems. There are many books written by Hicks as well as a wealth of tape recordings and videos, all easily accessed online.

Kryon is an entity who has never had a physical form in our planet, but gives us invaluable knowledge on how the earth was created, how our population was developed, and gives great detail of other civilization throughout our galaxy and beyond. He also teaches how we can communicate to our cells, what the nature of disease is and what we can do to overcome it, among many other practical issues.
He reiterates the fact that consciousness creates form, that we are not victim of circumstances that we are eternal beings, one with "source" and capable of transforming our world in ways that up to now we thought of as only dreams.
He states that we have been given perhaps the most awesome gift of all; the ability to project your thoughts into physical form, and that no objective reality exists but

that which is created by consciousness.
He further explains that when we come to
earth, we leave a part of our souls on the
other side of the veil, and that is part of
our souls. This part constitutes our Higher
Self which is in constant communication with
us but at a subconscious level, so we are
not aware of it. This is the part of our
soul that is responsible for our
synchronicities.
Kryon speaking about civilizations
throughout the universe says that highly
advanced civilizations such as the
Pleiadians, the Arcturians, and the ones
from the Orion Constellation no longer use
technology. They gave it up long ago because
everything they want to create, they create
out of consciousness.
He channels through Lee Carrol, an American
speaker and author. Kryon has authored
thirteen books on channeling through Carrol
and has coauthored three more books.

"A Course in Miracles" is a teaching,
channeled through Columbia University
psychologist Dr. Helen Schucman, during a
seven year period. She is a highly respected
research psychologist who heard a "voice"
dictating the material to her. Throughout
the entire project she was given assistance
and support by Dr. William N. Thetford, the
head of the Psychology Department in which
she worked. The course is a three-volume set

of books, a self-study course designed to
help change one's perception.
There are over two million copies in print.
The Course comprises perhaps the most
important writing in the English language
since the translation of the Bible. The
three books are: the text, the workbook for
students and the manual for teachers. The
workbook includes 365 lessons, one for each
day of the year. It deals with the same
psychological and spiritual truths as the
New Testament, but presented in a simple
form which has influenced hundreds of
thousands of lives throughout the planet.
I had gone through about a third of the text
before I realized that this Course must have
been channeled by Jesus, because he talks
about his crucifixion as, a "useless
journey." The emphasis, he says, was meant
to be in the resurrection, but since
humanity is so enamored with the concepts of
suffering, pain, revenge, and hate, it made
the cross the symbol of his existence. Later
on, I found out that in study groups, it is
known that it was in fact Jesus who dictated
it.
The Course teaches that the world we live in
is a vast illusion, and teaches what the
"real world" is and how to attain it. It
makes a fundamental distinction between the
real and the unreal; between knowledge and
perception.
It says:

>Nothing real can be threatened

>Nothing unreal exists.

>Herein lies the piece of God.

It is impossible to summarize the Course and I would not even consider enumerating the teachings, but it is highly recommend it to anyone who desires to know the truth of what we are, beyond the mask of the ego.

The last channeler that I will mention is Bashar, from whom I have learned many valuable lessons. Bashar is an Arabic word which means messenger. His messages are delivered through the channel Darryl Anka, an American movie producer and writer who lives in Los Angeles, CA. He has been channeling Bashar's messages for the past thirty years.
The first time I heard about Bashar I was very skeptical because I was told he is a member of the Sassanian civilization from the planet Essassani, said to exist about 500 light years away in the direction of the Orion constellation. It sounded to me as science fiction and did not pay much attention to it.
As I read more of his message however, I was intrigued. In his sessions, the attendants ask him questions about different subjects including personal problems. The way he answered them was very helpful to them. In

one occasion a scientist in the audience asked him questions about quantum physics and the structure of the atom, about which he had doubts, misconceptions and lack of understanding. The way in which the questions were answered, changed my mind about him. Obviously, this entity knew more than the scientist and the explanation given to him made a lot of sense.

Bashar says that it does not make any difference at all, whether people believe he was an ET or where he came from. He said if the information given to you helps you solve your problems and helps you live a happier and more balanced life that is what is important; the source of the information is irrelevant. I found the message compelling and became very interested in what he had to say.

One of the most valuable lessons that I learned is that what we consider disasters, tragedies, and accidents, are actually gifts in disguise, they are designed to teach us a lesson, otherwise they would have not occurred. They are a warning to us that something is amiss, and not in accord with what we really are. When we are confronted with such situations we generally tend to lose control, become stressed, and start asking questions like why does this happen to me, this is bad, this is a disaster, it should have never happened, and so on, not realizing the lesson to be learned from this unexpected experience.

If you see the gift in these events, says Bashar, you will spend the rest of your days "unwrapping gifts."

As with other channelers, Bashar teaches that the world we see around us is nothing but a reflection or mirror of our beliefs. We cannot change the world but we can change the way we see it. When you look at yourself in the mirror and you want the reflection to smile, you cannot go to it and try to make it smile, but if you smile, the mirror has no choice but to reflect that smile. The same occurs when we want to change whatever is it we don't prefer.

The problem in your world, says Bashar, is that you try to change what you don't like, and of course it does not work. You change your beliefs about it and your world will change. Physical reality actually is a mirror reflecting what you believe to be true, and will not change until you change your beliefs.

Everything is here and now, he says. Creation is done. When you want to create the reality you prefer, is not as if it has to be created out of nothing. This is not the case, he explains, the world you want to create already exists in some dimension of consciousness.

He also discusses parallel realities, a subject of which scientists are becoming aware, and several excellent books have been

written on this subject alone.
We change from parallel reality to parallel
reality billions of times per second. We are
generally not aware of this change because
the world we change to is very similar to
the previous one, with only minimal changes.
Movement, he explains, never actually takes
place; the changes from one world to the
next are so rapid that it gives you the
illusion of something moving. Is like a
movie film where static pictures are
projected on the screen at such speed that
it gives you the illusion of movement. When
you watch a movie, it is the rapid
succession of pictures which gives the
illusion of movement, and the same occurs in
the world.
According to him, we live in a multiple
universe reality but we are aware only on
the reality we are focused on. The other
ones remain invisible to us. He gives the
analogy of TV. There are hundreds of
channels all working simultaneously, but we
are aware only of the one we are watching.
If we are watching channel two, all other
channels are just as real but we are not
aware of what is taking place in them
because our awareness is in the frequency of
channel two. If we change to, say channel
five, we are aware of what is happening in
channel five but not of events in channel
two. If we want be aware of events in other
channels, all we need to do is to change to

94

the frequency of the desired channel.
But Bashar is not the only one who discusses
parallel universes. In our tangible world,
the first idea of parallel universes was
first conceived by Princeton University grad
student Hugh Everett, one evening in 1954.
He came up with the idea that the quantum
effect can cause the universe to constantly
split. He developed the idea for his PH.D
degree, and the theory has held up.
The proposal is that there could be
countless other universes besides our own,
where all the choices you make in this life
played out in alternate realities. An
analogy may clarify this. If you are offered
a job in China and another in The U.S., and
you finally make the decision to take the
one in the US, the energy you create in
considering the job in China, is not lost.
There is a version of you that took the job
in China, thus creating an alternate you in
a parallel or alternate universe of which
you are not aware because you are just
focused on the universe where you took the
job in the US. This theory would apply to
every decision we make about everything
else. The idea is that every time we make a
choice a parallel world is created.
Burt Goldman, who has been described as The
American Monk, has spent more than half a
century perfecting the art of meditation and
has been able to communicate with other
versions of himself. He teaches this art and

guides his students through a meditative state of consciousness where they can also contact other version of themselves to obtain information that helps them solve their problems. He describes the process as a sort of mental teleportation, and says that the multiverses are all around us but we are not fine-tuned to them.

Although the idea of parallel universes or multiverse at first appear nonsensical, gradually it has received more and more attention in the scientific community. Recently the MIT (Massachusetts Institute of Technology) made the statement that Everett's work is as important as Einstein's is on relativity.
In December 2017 a group of scientists said that new conception of quantum mechanics rests on the idea that parallel universes exists, and that they interact with our own. The bizarre effects of quantum mechanics that we observe and are confused by, such as the double slit experiment, are really caused by the interactions between these universes.   Many books on parallel universes called the multiverse have been written by scientists such as Alfred Wolf, Ph.D., and Michio Kaku, Ph.D., among many others.   Dr. Cynthia Sue Larson, has written extensively about alternative realities and quantum jumps. She has an online monthly newsletter on the

subject and has also written on her own experiences about quantum jumps and alternate parallel universes. Very recently, Cambridge University reported the most recent study by Stephen Hawking along with scientist Thomas Hertzog, in which they concluded that parallel universes are a certain possibility and that they follow the same physical laws of our universe. This was reported in the Journal of High Energy Physics.   I find it very interesting that all channelers I am aware of without exception, bring the same message, although in different ways, and in different form. They all tell us that we create our own reality, that the world we see is the reflection of our own belief system, that the world we see and we live in is not real, but an illusion.

As world lecturer and writer David Icke puts it "Love is the only reality, everything else is an illusion."

Chapter 8

The Astral World.

Most people are not familiar with the astral world, although they go there every night when they go to sleep.
Recently however, there seems to be a great interest in this plane of existence and there are countless videos and books on how to navigate and travel in it.
The astral world is basically a counterpart of the physical world, it interpenetrates it, but it vibrates at a much higher rate of speed, so it becomes invisible to the eye. Every object in the physical plane has a counterpart in the astral.
I find significant difficulty in describing it in adequate terms, mostly because of the lack of words in our language to describe what is not physical.
Basically, astral matter exists in several orders which correspond to orders in the physical plane; solid, liquid and gaseous, and each variety of physical matter attracts astral matter of corresponding density. Thus solid physical matter is interpenetrated by solid astral matter, liquid by liquid, and

gaseous by gaseous. Each plane occupies the same space but is entirely unaware of the other and in no way impedes the free movement of its counterpart.

There is reason to believe that electrons in the physical are nothing but astral matter, while scientist are still scrambling to figure out what electron are made of.

Our bodies of course, have their counterparts in the astral. In his book "The Astral Body" author A.E. Powell describes the appearance of the astral body this way: "In the undeveloped man the astral body is a cloudy, loosely organized and vaguely outlined mass of astral matter with great predominance of substance from the lower grades; it is gross, dark in color and dense.

By contrast, in the average moral and intellectual man the astral body is considerable larger, extending about eighteen inches in all directions, giving it a luminous quality to the whole, so the outline is clear and definite.

In the case of a spiritually developed man the astral body is still larger in size and composed of even finer particles giving a beautiful display of colors. The portion of the astral body that extends beyond the limits of the physical is usually termed the 'astral aura' which in ancient texts is described as a halo of luminous light, depicted is some of the pictures of saints.

During the sleep of the physical body, an undeveloped man leads a dreamy, vague existence in his relatively primitive astral body, remembering little or nothing of his sleep-life when he wakes up from sleep. In the case of a developed man, the life in the astral body is active, and useful and the memory of his activities in the astral may be retained on awakening from sleep.11

One of the first things a man learns to do in the astral is to travel in it with incredible speed, and to great distances from the asleep physical body.

Many people have trained themselves to be conscious in the astral. They leave their physical body behind and function in this plane without restrictions.

This is the world we enter when we go to sleep. The physical body is asleep but the astral detaches itself from the physical and is free to navigate in the astral and have different experiences.

On awakening from sleep, we generally have no memory at all of our activities but sometimes we have a vague recollection of them and we think we had a dream.

In many cases, a person can succeed in impressing knowledge in the physical mind from the astral world, without memory of where or how that knowledge was obtained. Many times we are working on a solution of a problem for some time and then suddenly one day we wake up with the solution.

An understanding of the astral body, of its possibilities and limitations, is helpful to understand the life into which we pass after physical death. The many kinds of "heavens," "hells" and purgatorial existences by followers of many religions, all make sense as soon as we understand the astral body and the astral world.

Knowledge of the astral helps us understand the so-called "occult" phenomena such as apparitions, what takes place in the séance room, non-physical methods of healing disease, knowledge of places never visited before, and other phenomena for which no apparent explanation exists.

When we experience what is called a lucid dream, what happens is that within the dream, we become aware that we are dreaming. What this means is that we are conscious that we are in the astral, and we can function without the restrictions of the physical body. We can go through walls, through the ceiling, through water and any other barriers. We can travel instantly to any place we desire. If we think for instance of Rome, we are instantly there, without "traveling in between."

I have experienced it myself many times and have kept a record of those experiences. It has always happened spontaneously during sleep time, and the excitement of this freedom is such, that frequently I find

myself back in bed, awake and frustrated.
I remember the first time it happened. I
became aware I was dreaming, and therefore
in the astral. I knew I could go through the
ceiling and as I floated in the air, was
reluctant to go through.
I finally made a decision to give it a try
and went right through the ceiling with no
difficulty at all. In another occasion I
found myself at the edge of a cliff, looking
down about 300 feet to the bottom. I figured
that if I was in the astral should be able
to just float. Since it was the first time
that I experienced this situation, I was
hesitant at first, but decided to do it.
It took all I got to jump, but to my
delight, I floated in the air. The
experience of freedom is absolutely
incredible, anything you desire appears
instantly, you can go instantly wherever you
want.
The experiences in the astral appear so
real, even more real than the physical, that
I cannot say how many times I have missed
the opportunity to explore it because of my
inability to recognize I was in the astral,
and found myself instead back in my bed,
awaken and dissatisfied. Many times I have
experienced walking on water and feeling
very proud of having achieved such capacity,
not realizing that I was in the astral,
therefore missing the opportunity to explore
it further.

The astral appears very real, more so than the physical. The colors are more intense, sounds are clearer, and objects appear even more solid than in the physical, and that is the reason for the difficulty I have found in recognizing it.

It takes what Dr. Baker calls a "critical faculty" (more about Dr. Baker later in this chapter) to recognize this state. Sometimes it takes noticing incongruence like seeing a person with three eyes, or seeing something out of the ordinary to be aware you are in the astral.

A visitor to the astral world will inevitably be impressed by the amount and variety of beings who inhabit it. Since there are seven planes of existence, there are different beings in each plain. In the upper level there are what the Hindus call "Devas," who are elsewhere spoken of as "Angels." According to A. E. Powell these beings belong to an evolution distinct from humans.

Just as there are Devas in the upper levels, in the lower levels are creatures like sylphs, nature spirits, gnomes, water spirits, air spirits, salamanders, which in popular language have been called ferries, pixies, elves, goblins, and many other names.

Their shapes vary, but are most frequently human in shape but diminutive in size. They can change their appearance at will and can make themselves visible by materialization when they want to be visible in the physical world, and this is what happens during séances, where they can answer questions, read minds of those present and play any number of tricks to amuse their audience. Out of body experiences (OBE) and near death experiences (NDE) all occur in the astral. People who have near death experiences relate very similar events. They seem to go through a long tunnel at the end of which they see a beautiful light, encounter luminous beings who welcome them and frequently tell them the time is not yet for them to remain there and that they have to go back as their experience on earth is not yet completed. At other times they are given the choice to remain there or go back. Upon being resuscitated, those people generally experience a significant personality change. They tend to become more relaxed, happier, more easygoing, and loving. These changes are frequently so dramatic that some of them appear to be a completely new person. Generally they become convinced of the immortality of the soul, and become more spiritual.

People who experience the astral plain find that they are able to create objects instantly just by thinking about them, including creation of new bodies.

People confined to wheelchairs in physical

existence find themselves walking and running in healthy bodies. The elderly can develop young strong bodies; amputees have their healthy limbs and move about without restrictions.

In the astral, vision is not limited to eye sight. They see what is behind, above below and in front of them.

NDEs frequently report being in the presence of beings of light, these are the Devas mentioned earlier, a hierarchy just above human.

The astral is not only the plain where some dreams take place. This is also the place where we go when we die. It is possible therefore to find our relatives or loved ones who have just passed on. The difference in the astral between a dead person and one having astral experience is that there is what has been called in eastern esoteric philosophies "the silver cord." This cord or life force is a thin string of light which connects the astral body to the physical. When we travel in the astral regardless of distance, the cord is intact but when we die, the cord is severed.

Emmanuel Swedenborg was a Swedish scientist, mathematician and mystic born in1768. He was a very well educated man, politician, astronomer, businessman and writer. He was referred to as the Leonardo da Vinci of Scandinavia. He spoke nine languages and had developed the ability to function consciously in the astral world, being able to communicate with the dead, spirits and angels, and was a man of great reputation. In one occasion the queen of Sweden asked him whether he would undertake a commission in regard to her lately deceased brother Augustus William of Prussia, who had died on June 12, 1758, a challenge Swedenborg was only too glad to accept. He promised her to consult with her deceased brother, and the next day he gave the queen information that was very secret, and according to her, only she and her brother could possibly know. Swedenborg became so well known that the German philosopher Immanuel Kant was inspired to write a book on him entitled "Dreams of a Spirit-Seer."

There are many more well-known personalities who have been able to voluntarily enter the astral. Lobsang Rampa, a Tibetan physician author of many fascinating books practiced this art, and this helped him cope with the harsh treatment and torture by the Japanese during World War II while prisoner in a concentration camp. He wrote extensively about the astral and how Tibetan monks practiced it routinely.
Helen Blavatsky founder of the Theosophical Society wrote and taught her students how to practice astral travel or astral projection, as is also called, and how to obtain

information in it to advance their careers
and solve their problems.

Robert Monroe, founder of the famous Monroe
Institute, had extensive experience in out
of body travel and remote viewing. When he
had his first out of body experience, he
found himself floating above his body, and
thought that for sure he was going crazy. He
immediately sought medical help, but the
doctors were unable to help him. It was not
until he read that yogis and shamans of
India had similar experiences that he
developed interest in studying this
phenomenon more in dept. He had significant
experience working consciously in the
astral. He founded the Monroe Institute
located in the Blue Ridge Mountains in the
state of Virginia where he conducts many
seminars. He has also written several books
on his out of body experiences.

In the 80's, I took a week long seminar at
the institute. In one of the meditation
exercises, I was suddenly in front of many
of my relatives who had died. They all look
happy, radiant and loving; they were all
positioned together in two rows like posing
for a photograph. My mother died when I was
only one year old, and I had seen her only
in pictures, but she looked somewhat
different, younger and prettier. My father
who had died just a few months earlier was
by her side, my older brother, uncle and
others were also present. They all looked

astonishingly real.

In another exercise, I had a very vivid experience. I saw myself in southern France, in a typical French army uniform, being shot to death in a war. I did not know what war or in what year, but remember clearly floating above my dead body and saying to myself: Wow! Therefore, you really survive death, what I have heard about life after death is true, this is great. The experience then disappeared just as suddenly as it came to me. I never knew what this experience meant. I don't know if it was a memory from a previous life time, all I know is that it appeared extremely real.

Perhaps the most notorious practitioner of activities in the astral in recent times was Dr. Douglas Baker, an English physician who died in 2011. He was the founder of the Claregate College in Potters Bar, England. He taught esoteric sciences and alternative medicine. Although the college no longer exists, the studies can be undertaken online with the Claregate Metaphysics Group. During his career spanning more than fifty years, he gave thousands of lectures and conducted hundreds of seminars on metaphysical subjects including astral travel. He wrote many books and did extensive research on dark matter, dark energy and quantum physics.

As a mystic, Dr. Baker was placed by his

master teacher, Robert Browning, known as "The English Master" in circumstances in which he had to play a part in the astral world consoling and directing victims of air crashes, sometimes in numbering scores. In one occasion, he writes, he remembered clearly a group of about fifty such victims where a plane had crashed into a hillside. They were gathered around the burning remains, huddled together and greatly astounded that they had survived. There was a lot of bewilderment and wailing. He tried to console the victims, but they were even more upset when he informed them that they were now dead and that they had obviously not survived in the physical, and should now take up their places in the astral world.12 People who die suddenly as in accidents or who are killed, generally do not realize they are dead. They enter the astral and this new world is every bit as real as the physical, so they don't realize they are dead.

Dr. Baker would go to bed at night, put his body to sleep, and with continuity of consciousness enter the astral where his work continued. In one occasion he confronted a young woman who had just died in a small plane crash. The plane she was in with relatives lost control and went down in the Alps. When he gently broke to her the news that she had just died, she felt insulted and became very angry. "Can't you

see we are talking? If I were dead that
would not be happening," she said, despite
the fact that she saw her mangled dead body.
She was convinced she had somehow survived
the crash and it took him a while to
convince her otherwise.

But this denial is not always the case. Dr.
George De La Warr, (founder of the well-
known laboratory which carries his name in
Oxford, England), was a good friend of Dr.
Baker's and the two frequently discussed
esoteric subjects and the astral world.
When he died, Baker found him in the astral.
"Do you realize you are now dead?" asked
Baker. Of course old chap, he replied, we
talked about it so many times, I am
perfectly aware of where I am. This was very
refreshing to Baker and rejoiced that his
work had been made easier.
In one of Baker's books "Life After Death"
he writes:
*After the Second World War, a period during
which the very nature of traumatic
experiences evoked in me astral awareness, I
observed the utter chaos that existed in the
astral world. The problem was that the young
British Tommies, the American GIs, as well
as the Germans and Italians, who had been
part of the armed forces in combat and now
dead, were unaware of their change of state.
The British and Americans still fought
Germans and Italians, and vice versa. There*

was pandemonium everywhere.

He describes in his books on the subject of alcoholism, the fate of those alcoholics who take their own lives, only to find themselves still earthbound by their attraction towards alcohol and its fumes. They hang out in bars and since they do not have the capacity to drink as in the physical, they do whatever they can to be able to drink alcohol and occasionally if they find someone in the physical who has passed out from excessive alcohol drinking, they try to possess that individual to be able to drink again.

He points out that one of the main difficulties alcoholics experience trying to recover from it, or to "dry out" is the constant vampirism upon the individual by astral entities who had once been themselves alcoholics.

I had the opportunity to meet Dr. Baker in many of his trips to the Washington DC area in the 70s and 80s and discussed with him his extensive experiences. He had a large group of students and taught esoteric subjects for many years.

In one of his many lectures he told us that most people don't know they are dead. When questioned, they are generally most surprised even indignant, at the suggestion that they are dead. When their attention is directed to certain differences that exist

111

in the astral, they eventually acknowledge
that something has happened, some "change"
has taken place, they may be altered in some
way, but not dead.
Dr. Baker's case is not unique. Highly
developed and advanced persons who have
continuity of consciousness between the
astral and physical lives, no longer have
days of consciousness and nights of
oblivion, and become instead a continuous
whole year after year of unbroken
consciousness. When they die, they just
continue their work only in the astral.

Chapter 9

Reincarnation

> *"It ain't what you don't know that gets you in trouble*
>
> *It is what you know for sure that ain't so."*

Mark Twain

The subject of survival of the human personality after the death of the body, has been prominent among the questions which philosophers, researchers and spiritual teachers have tried to explain and understand.

Reincarnation is the belief that we live not just one life but many lives, the concept that the soul adopts a new physical body and returns to the physical world at some point after discarnate existence.

Reincarnation is for most people, a very difficult subject, mainly because so much nonsense and silliness have been written and talked about, that many people dismiss it off hand.

No evidence can be a proof that reincarnation exists, and it is certainly not the intention of this chapter to proof that it is so. The findings that are mentioned here are presented as intriguing possibility and to be considered with an open mind, without preconceived notions and ideas that living only one life is the only possibility.

Reincarnation is the backbone of the teachings of the Rosicrucian's, the Theosophical Society (created by Helen Blavatsky) and taught by many religions such as the Hindu. In the East over 600 million people accept this concept and incorporate this teaching in their daily lives.

It was also taught by some of the most eminent thinkers of antiquity such as Pythagoras, Plato, Plotinus, Socrates and others and has thence infiltrated into most western cultures.

More recently with the developing interest of oriental philosophy, large numbers of westerners are finding it the only rational basis for continuing to live in conditions of stress and many inequalities of opportunity, birth, health and wealth which living in the West presents.

To my knowledge, the earliest investigation of someone remembering a past life occurred in India, in the eighteen century. The Mogul

Emperor of the time, hearing of a case where
a man started taking about injuries
inflicted on him in a previous life, became
interested in it and had the witness brought
before him so he could interrogate him
directly. He was amazed at the accuracies.
The man had features such as birthmarks,
which corresponded to injuries in a previous
life.
Do we really survive death? Dr. Ian
Stevenson, professor and head of child
psychiatry at the University of Virginia
interviewed more than three thousand
children from all over the world who
remembered having lived before, often in
great detail.
This monumental research took Dr. Stevenson
more than forty years to complete. He wrote
a book "Twenty Cases Suggestive of
Reincarnation." These were cases that he
himself investigated directly, visiting
foreign countries, interviewing surviving
relatives, tracking down neighbors and
friends of the person they claimed to be in
a previous life.
One girl from Lebanon remembered the full
names and relationships of twenty- five
different people from her alleged past life.
In another case, a boy who said he had
committed suicide in a previous life by
shooting himself in the head, had birth
marks in his head which lined up perfectly
along the bullet's trajectory.

Another physician who became interested in
past life memories is Jim B. Tucker, MD,
professor of psychiatry and neurobehavioral
sciences at the University of Virginia. He
continued the work of Dr. Stevenson, and
authored the book "Life After Life." He has
spent a decade studying cases of children
who remember a past life. He has found cases
that provide persuasive evidence that some
children do in fact possess memory of
previous lives. A boy who described a life
in a small island was investigated by
Tucker, who found details that matched the
boy's statements.
Another boy pointed at a photograph from the
1930's and said he used to be one of the men
on it. Once the laborious effort to identify
that man was successful, many of the child's
numerous memories were found to match the
details of his life. A third boy began
expressing memories of being a pilot in
World War II. The pilot was eventually
identified.
Many of the children had birthmarks or
birthing defects in the exact location where
their former selves had been mortally
wounded. David Wilcock author of many
excellent books, professional lecturer and
researcher of consciousness writes that if
our new physical bodies bear a strong facial
resemblance to who we were before, this
suggests that there is an energetic aspect
to who we are, as humans that carries over

from one lifetime to another, and that this energetic aspect which he refers to as the soul, is able to shape and mold our facial features as well as re-create a mortal wound with a birthmark or deformity.

Children in general appear to be more likely to remember past lives in cultures that believe in reincarnation, so parents who do not embrace the notion of reincarnation may be missing a great opportunity when their children begin to talk about unusual memories.

The legendary American psychic Edgar Cayce, the "Sleeping Prophet" was able to enter a self-induced trance, and in this trance was able to describe in detail the medical and mental problems of his clients. He was very accurate in diagnosing medical conditions and recommending effective treatments with amazing good results, in cases where conventional medicine had given up. He never charged for his services and was so successful, that a group of businessmen built for him a hospital in Virginia Beach, VA. He gave thousands of readings and practiced medical diagnosis by clairvoyance for forty-three years. He also gave spiritual advice and vocational guidance when these were specifically requested. During the depression years, the business men who were supporting the hospital operations, were no longer able to afford

the expense and were obligated to close it.
Today in the same place where the hospital
once stood, a modern building was erected,
the ARE (Association for Research and
Enlightenment). There are in the building
records of over 14,000 readings along with
the most complete collection of esoteric
literature in the country. They feature a
daily conference on subjects related to the
Edgar Cayce's work.
One time in 1923, while giving a reading to
one of his clients, information started to
come about events in previous lives. Cayce,
being a devote Christian became very
concerned because Christians do not believe
in reincarnation and this information
created such crisis in his life, that for a
while he stopped giving readings.
Over time, he came to accept reincarnation,
as his readings gave detailed information
about many of his client's past lives.
According to his readings, the average
person that came to him had as many as forty
past lives.
In many instances knowledge of previous
lives brought complete relief of the
physical and mental conditions of his
clients. In one such occasion a young man
came to see him because he was afflicted
with severe upper back pain for many years
and his doctors after running all kinds of
tests available at the time, had been unable
to diagnose his condition or relieve his

pain. During the reading, he was told that in a previous life he was working at the famous Alexandria Library when it burned down. When the fire broke out, he was busy with his work, and when he became aware of the fire, tried to escape, but was not able to get out on time and a large heavy object came down hitting him on the back and killed him. After the client was aware of this episode his back pain gradually disappeared over the next few days, never to come back again.

During the past few years, many psychiatrists have been using hypnosis to access memories from previous lives to cure phobias, and other conditions not responding to conventional known methods. One of these is Dr. Brian Weiss, Head of the Psychiatry department at Mount Sinai Medical Center in Miami, FL and Associate Clinical Professor of Psychiatry at Miami University Medical School, Miami, FL. Dr. Weiss started using hypnosis and age regression to investigate painful episodes during childhood that might shed a light on the current symptoms experienced by his patients. He did not believe in reincarnation and like most psychiatrists, practiced orthodox, conventional medicine. But In one occasion, he treated a patient whom he calls Catherine, who under hypnosis started talking about her experiences in previous lives, some going back from 1863 BC to 1568 BC. In one of the previous lives, Catherine drowned in a tsunami that hit the town where she lived. After she was aware of this memory of her traumatic death, her fear of drowning disappeared as well as other symptoms.

Dr. Weiss, a former skeptic, became convinced that reincarnation was something that deserved attention and after thousands of regressions to previous lives, he became a lecturer on the subject of reincarnation and conducts seminars and workshops where he instructs the students on the art of hypnosis and past life regression.

He is the author of "Many Masters Many Lives" (Touch Stone, NY 1988), and several other books.

Many patients under hypnosis speak in foreign languages not known to them in the present life. Many describe historic facts and detailed geographic locations which are not known to them in their awake state.

Dr. Michael Newton, the author of several books on reincarnation is another physician who has made a towering contribution on the subject of past life regressions. He is one of the most influential past life researchers. He became a specialist in treating a variety of psychological disorders using hypnotic suggestion, a technique he used to change habitual patterns.

As in the case of Dr. Weiss, Dr. Newton was a skeptic and did not believe in reincarnation or the afterlife.

His belief system began to change while working with a young man who had experienced chronic pain in the right side of his chest throughout his entire life. Under hypnosis the man told him, without any hesitation that he had been stabbed to death with a bayonet while fighting in World War 1 in France. This case was the beginning of his significant experience in past life regression.

In his first book "Journey of Souls" he describes ten distinct stages a soul goes through from initial death to the time of reincarnation, from "Death and departure" to "Rebirth," based on what he learned from many patients at different stage of the afterlife.

Another therapist of great renown was Dolores Canon, a regressive hypnotherapist and psychic researcher, born in St Louis, Missouri. In 1968 she had her first exposure to reincarnation via regressive hypnosis when her husband, an amateur hypnotist, stumbled through a past life while working on a patient who had consulted him about weight loss. She studied various hypnosis methods and eventually developed her own technique which led her to quickly take her subjects to a deep trance and get accurate information from her subjects.

She has written more than ten books based on her own experiences. What I find interesting about Dolores and makes her work unique is that she not only obtained information to help her patients with health issues, but she got extensive information through her past life regressed patients on UFOs, extraterrestrial civilizations, quantum physics, parallel universes, and through the unconscious mind of her subjects she had direct communication with Nostradamus, from which she wrote "Conversations with Nostradamus," Volumes I, II and III. In her recent book "Convoluted Universe" (Ozark Mountain Publishers, first print in 2001). She obtained significant information from a patient regarding parallel universes, the mystery of the pyramids, Atlantis, the Nazca Lines in Peru and other unsolved mysteries. One more feature of Ms. Cannon's practice which was uncommon was the capacity to talk directly to the subconscious mind of her subjects just like if she were to another person, and this fact gave her the opportunity to really be of benefit to her clients.

Dr. Joel L. Whitton, a professor of psychiatry at the University of Toronto Medical School, has also used hypnosis to investigate previous lives. He has spent thousands of hours recording what his patients remembered about their alleged previous existences.

In one case, one man had an inexplicable British accent as a child and an irrational fear of breaking a leg, a persistent nail-biting habit, an obsessive fascination with torture, and as a teenager had a vision of being in a room with a Nazi officer. Under hypnosis the patient recalled being a pilot in World War II. He recalled being shot down while on a mission over Germany. He recalled having his plane hit by a shower of bullets, one of them penetrated his leg and broke it, causing him to lose control of the plane and forcing him to crash-land. He was captured by the Nazis, brutally tortured, had his fingernails pulled out, and eventually died in prison.13

Scientist are beginning to take a serious look at these cases, and we as a society have much to gain from research into the mysteries of the mind, the soul, the continuation of life after death and the influence that past life knowledge can have on our present life experience.

Apparently there were many references in the New Testament about reincarnation. In the year A.D.325 the Roman Emperor Constantine, who was a very wise man and was tired of fights between Christians and Pagans, wanted once and for all to have the Church be more in control on the people. To this effect, and with the help of his mother Helen, he convened the famous Council of Nicaea. Anything that he interpreted not in his best interest was thrown out of the New Testament, including every passage suggestive of reincarnation. He did not want for his people to think that if they failed in this life they had another chance in the next life.

When Emperor Theodosius made Christianity the sole and official religion of the state in A.D.395, the institution assumed complete control over individual minds and humanity entered the thousand year period referred as the Dark Ages.

By A.D. 553, the Roman government officially declared that it was illegal to believe in or to teach the concept of reincarnation. Any failure to abide by this law in those days would mean almost certain death.

Because of the changes made by Constantine, the New Testament could be called accurately Constantine's New Testament.

The early church fathers had accepted the concept or reincarnation. The Gnostics, Clement of Alexandria, Saint Jerome and others believed they had lived before.

During my years of medical practice I had the opportunity to hear from patient's accounts of their near death experiences also known as NDEs. One such case occurred when I was on call on a weekend. On Saturday morning, I was making rounds at the hospital. A patient of one of my partners developed a cardiac arrest and had to be resuscitated and I was present during efforts by the emergency team to bring him back to life. After the defibrillator was used, his heart started beating, vital signs returned but he remained unconscious. The next day I came to see him, and instead of finding a grateful patient, he was angry. He asked me what right we had to bring him back to life. It took me a while to come up with an acceptable answer. Once he settled down and regained composure he told me he had an extraordinary experience "On the other side." He proceeded to describe how he floated above his body and watched how nurses and doctors worked furiously to bring him back. He described the whole episode with great accuracy, just as if I had witnessed it. He told me I was there but did not see me participating in the effort. I don't remember his exact words but he told me he found himself in the light with luminous people welcoming him. He said that for the first time in his life he experienced true love and that he was at total peace in a place so beautiful he could not describe it. He was told that he could stay there if he wanted, but just as this was happening, suddenly he was awake in bed with tubes in every orifice of his body, with pain everywhere, puzzled by the experience. He was not a religious man, but was deeply moved and changed by his experience. Unlike other cases of NDE, he did not enter a tunnel but otherwise his experience was typical of people who were clinically dead but brought back to life.

The entire medical profession is trained to keep people alive despite their suffering, rather than keeping them comfortable, so they can die with dignity. To us in the medical field death is a failure. To a relative, it may be a disaster, but to the soul it is a release, and end to suffering and a culmination of one more mission accomplished.

"Death is not an error, it is not a failure

It is removing a very tight shoe"

Ram-Dass

Many times despite our efforts, the patient dies, because once the soul makes a decision to drop the body, nothing we do will change that.
Many people argue that reincarnation makes good sense, because if we live after death, then surely we must have lived before, and as the number of lives play such an important role in spiritual development it is unlikely we would just be given one chance at it.

Dr. Douglas Baker mentioned in the previous chapter, who had extensive experience dealing with the dead, wrote that homosexuality is generally the result of many consecutive lives in the opposite sex. If for example a man in present life has had many previous lives as a woman, the feminine aspect of his personality is so strong that is still prevalent in this life. Basically, he is still a woman, now in the body of a man, and it may take more than one life to gradually make the transition.

In my medical career I have read of some possible causes of homosexuality, but none makes much sense. Dr. Baker's however not only makes good sense, but appears to go to the root of the situation.

The very first time I ever heard of reincarnation was when I was sixteen years old. I visited my aunt Natalie who was a member of the Theosophical society. One of the basic teachings of the Theosophical Society is the subject of reincarnation. She explained to me that we come to earth just as children go to school, with the purpose of learning. There is so much to learn, that you cannot learn it all at one time. You cannot teach Algebra to a child, she taught; it has to be a gradual process. You go to first grade, then there is a time off or vacation before you go to second grade, then to third, and so on. Just like children go

to school, we come to earth to learn in
several stages, she explained.
When our physical body no longer serves us
or is too sick and no longer useful, we
discard it. "To give you an example", she
said, "It is sort of like your overcoat. You
have used it, it has represented you well,
and you have taken good care of it, but
eventually it began to look old, went out of
fashion, became shiny, and you realized it
no longer served you, so you got rid of it
and you started looking for a new one. What
happens to the old coat after that does not
matter to you."
"In a similar way," she continued, "After
our physical body dies, we set it aside. We
review what we have done and learned, and
with the help of masters and beings of light
and counselors we plan our next life, based
on what we need to learn and what Karma we
have incurred (*karma* is Sanskrit word
meaning cause and effect). For instance, if
we have abused others, we may like to learn
what it feels like to be abused, if we
deprive someone from his freedom, we may
like to experience what is like having your
freedom taken away. You choose what
conditions would give you the best
opportunity to experience the lessons you
need to learn.
A baby may be born in the Buckingham Palace,
with all of his needs met, a loving family,
and all served to him in a silver platter,

while at the same time a baby is born to a socially underprivileged homeless and destitute woman. This child will have a hard time surviving. Do you think this is justice? There are children who are born with marked disabilities, while others are born with perfectly healthy ones. Do you think this is justice? There is no injustice in the universe, she taught. It is just the law of cause and effect in operation. The law of karma enforces retribution: evil actions undertaken in previous lives must be neutralized by good actions taken in lives to come. On the other hand cruelties committed are ameliorated by similar actions suffered in this and other lives. That is the reason for the statement in the Bible of "an eye for an eye and a tooth for a tooth." My aunt's explanation made sense, and I decided to look further into this possibility.

During the course of a retreat at the Monroe Institute in the Blue Mountains in Virginia, a participant asked one of the instructors a question about what happens after death. The instructor answered with an example. He said: "If you want to explore the depth of the ocean and you want to see what is in there, you cannot just dive in, you will be dead within minutes. You need SCUBA diving equipment, oxygen tank, and all necessary equipment. When you get done, that is, when

you are satisfied that you are finished with your exploration, you come out. Once you are out, you cannot continue to have your gear with you. You have to get rid of it, otherwise you cannot function. In the same way, when you have lived your life, you cannot continue with your physical body, you need to set it aside. You don't die, you just discard the body, because where you go it is not necessary. Just as you are not your SCUBA gear, you are not your body, you just set it aside."
I found this example very intriguing.

Chapter 10

Extraterrestrial Contact

"The signs are increasing

The lights in the sky will appear

Red, hue, green, rapidly.

Someone is coming from far away and

Want to meet the people of earth.

Meetings have already taken place,

But those who have really seen have

Been silent"

Pope John Paul XXIII

This is a subject that evokes a huge emotional response with most people. We are so accustomed to believe that in the entire universe, tiny earth is the only planet capable of sustaining life, that any challenge to this belief is met with skepticism, great resistance, and with some people plain disgust.

When we look at the night sky, we see multiple stars, some of which are far away entire galaxies and we wonder if we are alone in the universe. Is it possible that all these stars are there just to give us on earth an awesome spectacle at night?

Let us consider our universe. In our Milky Way galaxy alone there are about two hundred billion stars. Most of these stars are suns much larger than our sun with multiple planets orbiting around them. There are billions upon billions of galaxies in the universe, and as one astronomer wrote: there are more suns in the universe than grains of sand in all the beaches on planet earth.

In 2009, Dr. Alan Boss of the Carnegie Institute of Science speculated that there could be 100 billion earth-like planets in our Milky Way alone, capable of sustaining life.

Scientists frequently speak about the end of the universe, but is there really an end to it? If so, what lies beyond it? Our human mind is simply not capable of grasping concepts such as eternity, or infinity.

There have been numerous reports of UFOs (Unidentified Flying Objects) throughout history. Paintings dating back to antiquity depict flying objects, some of which

132

resemble airplanes and flying discs.

The Bible has numerous passages in reference to UFOs.

Perhaps one of the most notorious was the fascinating story of Ezekiel specially when looked at through the lens of modern technology. His "vision" of the Merkabah or wheeled chariot, is more likely to be a spaceship or space shuttle used by an advanced species to reach out to humans. Erich Von Däniken is one of the biggest proponents of this theory, providing a very compelling argument for an alternative interpretation of the Book of Ezekiel. His interpretation was so compelling that his theory even reversed the entire thesis of a NASA scientist book aimed at disproving his claim. In his book "Chariots of the Gods," he explains that Ezekiel's vision was that of a space shuttle, rather than a divine chariot.

Ezekiel describes seeing a wheeled chariot descend toward him from the sky, piloted by beings with the "likeness of a man." While many biblical versions of the story describe the being on a chariot as God, Von Däniken points out that the original Hebrew version never mentions God, this word was added later. Ezekiel even describes the fire powering the chariot as appearing as "glowing metal."

The prophet Elijah was another human taken to "heaven" in a space vehicle; his follower

Elisha was with him at the time and witnesses this, and in Kings, Chapter 2, Verse 11, reads: "And it came to pass, they (Elijah and Elisha) still went on, and behold, there appeared a chariot of fire and horses of fire, and parted them both asunder; and Elijah went up by a whirlwind into heaven." Obviously the chariots and horses represent a vortex of energy.

The prophet Zechariah gave a very precise description of a UFO, in chapter 5, Verses 1-2 "Then I turned up mine eyes and looked, and behold, a flying scroll. And he said unto me, "What seest thou?" I answered, "I see a flying scroll, the length thereof is 20 cubits, and the breath thereof 10 cubits." This suggests a cigar- shape type of flying object.

There are other sources of information from Biblical times. One of them is contained in the "Dead Sea Scrolls" which were discovered in 1947 in a series of twelve caves around the site known as Wadi Qumran, near the Dead Sea, in the West Bank of the Jordan River. They were found by a shepherd boy who accidentally discovered into large containers holding the scrolls, while trying to find one of his goats that had escaped. These scrolls contained a wealth of information regarding the Biblical times, as well as practices and beliefs of ancient Judaism. Conventional wisdom tells us that they were written by a breakaway Jewish sect called the Essenes, between 150 B.C. and 70 AD. These scrolls were written mostly in Hebrew, but some in Sanskrit and Greek. These scrolls are kept in heavily guarded sites in a Jerusalem.

Frank E. Stranges founder of the National Investigation Committee on UFOs, before his death in 2008, spoke publicly for the first time about the classified information contained in some of those scrolls. He stated that the scrolls made it clear UFOs and extraterrestrials do exist and are real. According to the Dead Sea Scrolls, one of the passages of the Bible in connection to the journey of the Hebrews through the Sinai Desert reads: "A huge flying spacecraft capable of producing light and fire," instead of what says in the Bible "A cloud by day and a pillar of fire by night," which has a totally different meaning.
The Scrolls also state that Ezekiel was taken by a spacecraft to Venus, and that on the way back he was anointed with oils from Venus and Jupiter.
According to Dr. Stranges, the Scrolls also mention that before Adam, there was a civilization which became very advanced in sciences, economy, arts, literature and technology, and that they had reached high levels of intelligence which made them capable of building rockets that took them to other planets. As time went by, a wave of

distrust and hate developed and they ended up destroying themselves.

Stranges stated that the Bible has been intentionally altered, to keep the truth from becoming known.
There have been seventy two English versions of it, and from 1944 to 1993 alone, more than fifty versions were produced.
In biblical times, anyone coming down from the sky would obviously be a God, and they spoke about gods coming from heaven and intermingled with humans, creating Demi-Gods.
No matter how far out our belief in extraterrestrials may seem to some people, the fact is that belief in their existence has become both widespread and more accepted.
In an issue of Popular Mechanics, Kenneth Nealson, a scientist on the National Academy of Sciences Subcommittee for Solar System Exploration, said, "The search of life is no longer a fringe type of thing.[14] There have been innumerable reports of UFO sightings from all over the world, literally thousands of encounters with UFOs and hundreds of books written on this subject, as well as claims of abductions carried out by occupants of these vehicles. UFOs have been watched on radar screens to make instant ninety-degree-angle turns while traveling at incredible speeds, something that would rip

a physical object apart. They can change size, shape, and color, can instantly vanish into nothingness, and do other bizarre actions which have researchers scratching their heads.

Many theories have been proposed to explain what they are and many researchers have postulated that they are not objective but subjective, and holographic in nature. Michael Talbot, the author of the holographic Universe coined the term "omnijective" indicating that they are not objective or subjective, but probably more than that, or a combination of both. Scientists have great difficulty considering the possibility of these objects being extraterrestrial, because of the vastness of the distance to other solar systems. But as Bashar puts it: "we are there, and then we are here, without traveling in between." This is called teleportation, a phenomenon poorly understood even by the most brilliant minds of our time. Scientists have teleported atoms for only short distances and not without significant effort. This phenomenon is without doubt a quantum jump beyond our current understanding.

The purpose of this chapter is not to create one more theory or to add to the mystery of the UFO enigma, but rather to review some of the facts that have been kept from us behind a thick wall of well-orchestrated secrecy.

A 2000 USA Today survey revealed that 43 percent of Americans believe UFOS are real.15 Astronaut Gordon Cooper wrote "I believe that these extraterrestrial vehicles and their crews are visiting this Lancet from other planets and are obviously more advanced that we are here on earth… Also, I did have occasion in 1951 to have two days of observation of many flights of them (UFOs), of different sizes, flying in higher formation, generally from east to west over Europe."16

There is no question that UFOs and ETs are real but there has been a systematic and well-orchestrated cover up which is the highest top secret in the history of the US, greater than the Manhattan Project, which dealt with the atomic bomb. Since the early 1940's the government has successfully created misinformation, depicting comic flying saucers with tiny little green men to produce an aura of ridicule around the subject. This program has been so successful that even to this date, many serious citizens including members of the military and police force are reluctant to report UFO encounters for fear of being ridiculed, and no one wants to be in that position. President Jimmy Carter had a UFO sighting while Governor of Georgia. This is what he wrote: "I don't laugh at people anymore who say they've seen UFOs. I have seen one myself."

In October, 1969, Carter had the astonishing
UFO encounter. During his 1976 campaign he
made a bold statement: "If I become
president, I will make every piece of
information this country has about UFO
sightings available to the public and the
scientists."
His intentions behind this statement were in
part what caused him to lose his re-
election. When he was about to address the
nation and fulfill his promise, according to
UFO researcher Dr. Steven Greer, he was told
by secret agents: "Mr. Carter, if you want
to finish your first term in office, you
keep your mouth shut."
Dr. Steven Greer is an MD, who gave up his
lucrative career as chief of Emergency
Medicine in a hospital in Asheville, North
Carolina, to dedicate his life to the
research of UFOs and extraterrestrial
intelligence. He is recognized as one of the
world's most respected authority on UFO and
extraterrestrial intelligence research. He
is a courageous man who has unmasked the
"Secret Government" which according to him
is the institution really in charge of the
U.S., not the president and congress, as we
have been lead to believe. His research has
taken him to many countries, and has
contacted many foreign governments
interested in exploring extraterrestrial
life. While in France, he invited several
high ranking government officials to witness

an UFO sighting, which took place successfully. He has contacted members of Congress, heads of the Joined Armed Forces Staff, high Pentagon officials and has briefed presidents of US, heads of States and Prime Ministers about ET Contact, UFO activities, and about the incredible acts of those who continue to enforce the biggest cover up in history.

He presented at the Press Club in Washington DC a group of military officers from all branches of the Armed Services, as well as members of the Police and Security Guards. These are people that we respect and trust with our protection. One by one of the members of this group testified about their encounters with UFOs, and in the case of many of them, their contact and interactions with extraterrestrial creatures. This group of witnesses have manifested their intention to repeat under oath, before congress, the testimony given at the Press Club.

In Dr. Greer's Close Executive Summary Briefing for members of Congress and VIPs in May, 2001, one of the witnesses who stood out the most was Sergeant Clifford Stone, who had worked on crash retrieval projects. He was so traumatized by the things he had witnessed in the line of duty that he burst into tears and almost could not finish his presentation. He had a field manual describing fifty-seven varieties of ET intelligent life now visiting earth.

Dr. Greer has written several compelling
books on the subject and has given
innumerable lectures which are available
online.

In a videotaped lecture on Nov 15, 2015, he
presented documents showing how
extraterrestrial contact has been taking
place since the 40's and how the government
has systematically placed a veil of secrecy
on all UFO activities and ET contact. He
also explains how the government has had
knowledge of levitation, methods of
propulsion without the use of fossil fuels
and free energy devices since the 40's but
this information has been kept a secret.17

In 1992 Dr. Greer was offered a billion
dollars to discontinue his research and
activities, which he refused. Since then,
several attempts have been made on his life.

Dr. Greer periodically brings people to
witness UFO encounters and has a wealth of
photographs and videotapes to support his
activities. He has personally had many
contacts with different civilizations
including inhabitants of the Andromeda
Galaxy.

I know that this claims appear as fiction,
but they are real and anyone can access all
this information through Dr. Greer's online
recordings and his "Sirius Disclosure"
project.

Following the World War II, the only
squadron in the world that had atomic

weapons was based in Roswell, NM. There was great UFO activity reported in that area. Three UFOs crashed close to Roswell in July, 1947, creating big news, and local newspapers reported the crashes. Within hours however, the Air Force was in charge and made them change the original story. Military personnel visited all the news media outlets that had received the original "flying saucer" press release, and demanded it back. Base commander William Blanchard's original flying saucer press statement was withdrawn and General Ramsey, Major Marcel and others appear on press release photographs with the made up story that the crashed disc was a misidentified weather balloon and nothing else. William Cooper in his book "Behold a Pale Horse" states that the radio station owner who had broadcasted the news, was called from Washington DC by both Nevada senator Dennis Chavez and a Federal Communication Commission official and warned not to broadcast the interview he had with a witness Mack Brazel who not only had personally seen the wreckage but had pieces of the metal recovered from the crash. Brazel was in fact held incommunicado for the next six days, after which he was accompanied by U.S. Army personnel to the radio station to publicly change the story and say that what he had found was just a weather balloon. Security was very tight and nobody was allowed at the site.

The press release by General Ramsey that the crashed disc was a misidentified weather balloon and nothing else marked the end of the Roswell story and there was no public interest for the next thirty years.
Later it has been documented that in fact three UFOs had crashed, and it has been speculated that the high power of the sophisticated radar systems interfered with their navigation system and caused them to lose control and crash. It was confirmed by Thomas Dubose retired Air Force brigadier general that General Ramsey had received orders from Washington DC to provide a cover up story. It has also been known that the bodies of the crew were recovered, one of them still alive, and taken to Los Alamos via Kirkland Air Force Base in Albuquerque, to Wright Patterson Field in Dayton Ohio.

President Truman and his commanding officers were stunned and virtually impotent to explain the incredible events that defied belief. President Truman created several groups to investigate the issue further. The CIA was then formed by presidential Executive Order, first as CIG (central Intelligence Group) which later became the CIA after the National Security Act was passed. It was created with the specific purpose of dealing with the alien presence. A special group of America's top scientists was organized under the name Project SIGN in

Dec, 1947 to study this phenomenon which later became project GRUDGE one year later. The CIA was greatly enhanced through the operation "Paper Clip." Through this operation, hundreds of Nazi scientists were brought from Germany. Many of this scientists had experience with antigravity and had experience with UFOs. One of the most prominent scientists was Werner von Braun, aerospace engineer who had pioneered the Nazi V-2s and was a great help to NASA with the space program.

Later, on Nov. 4, 1952 President Truman created the NSA (National Security Agency) by Executive Order with the primary purpose to decipher the alien communication language and study a dialogue with ETs. One of the most important groups created by President Truman under the advice of Secretary of Defense James Forrestal in 1947 was called the Majestic 12 or MJ 12, composed of some of the most brilliant minds to investigate these activities. The committee, as time went by became very extensive, grew out of government control, and eventually become what is known as the Military Industrial Complex (MIC) a huge institution which is completely autonomous, responds to no one, not even to the President or to Congress. President Truman kept the allies including the Soviet Union well informed of the alien situation, in case the ET turned out to be a threat to the human race, to defend the

144

planet in case of an invasion. In order to coordinate all efforts and keep it secret from the press, the Bilderberg Group was created which evolved into a part of the secret World Government that controls everything.

President Eisenhower in his farewell address to the nation in 1962 as President Kennedy was inaugurated, stated: "Beware if the Military Industrial Complex, it is the greatest threat to our democracy." He knew that this unconstitutional, illegal and corrupted group was totally out of hand and completely autonomous in their obscure activities.

This shadowy government is known to keep ET contacts and UFO activity in strict secrecy. Members of this paramilitary groups witnessing ET contact are sworn into the highest level of secrecy, and violation of this would be their death sentence. Many of them, old and no longer affected by threats because they were ill and near death have spoken publicly about what they have seen and done.

Several types of UFOs are man-made, in fact many of the sightings reported mainly in connection with abductions and cow mutilations are man-made. According to Dr. Greer the difference between a real ET UFO and man-made UFO is that the man-made have seams and rivets while no such things are present in the E.T's.

These man-made UFOs are piloted by biological robots which are made to look and walk like E.Ts, with the purpose of creating misinformation and fear, to advance their sinister agenda.

Dr. Greer author of The Sirius Disclosure has been warning us that this mysterious government has been trying to orchestrate a fake ET attack, to create panic, to justify increased expenditure in space weapons, and to accelerate the One World military power which is part of the "New World Order" plan.

The secrecy regarding this issue has been so enforced that when President Carter asked the transition CIA director George Bush Sr. to inform him of the secrets files of UFO and ET contacts, he refused to give him the information and asked him to get it elsewhere. Carter eventually contacted The Vatican, but although they did not deny possessing the information they would not give it to him.

Further evidence of the degree of secrecy is given by Dr. Greer in his book "Hidden Truth- Forbidden Knowledge." When Vice President Humphrey went to Kirkland AFB and Sandia Laboratory so he could learn about the secret UFO projects, and ET reverse engineering, he was told: "Sir, you are not allowed into this area. If you proceed further, we shoot to kill." This was done to the Vice President of the US!

When President Bill Clinton was asked by a
well-known news broadcaster why he had not
told people the truth about ET life, he
responded "there is a government within
government and I don't control it"
Mr. William Colby ex-director of CIA had
arranged a meeting with Dr. Greer to show
him evidence of antigravity and a free
energy device. Before the meeting took
place, Mr. Colby was found dead, floating in
the Potomac River in Washington DC.
There is a documentary film available on
Netflix "Unacknowledged," an expose of the
world's biggest secret, which is an
excellent summary of some of the events
mentioned in this chapter.

Milton William Cooper author of the book
"Behold a Pale Horse," mentioned earlier,
had received the highest degree of security
Clearance in the US navy. He participated in
many of the cover up operations and decided
to break the secrecy in 1989. In his book
he states that between 1/1947 and 12/1952
sixteen alien crafts crashed or were downed,
sixty five bodies recovered, one of which
was still alive. Of the sixteen crashes,
thirteen took place within the US borders,
one in Arizona, eleven in New Mexico, and
one in Nevada. The other three remaining,
crashed, one in Norway and two in Mexico.
He also states in his book that during
President Dwight Eisenhower first year in

office in 1953 at least ten crashing discs were recovered, with twenty six members of the crew dead and four alive. They were taken to what is now called Area 51, a very tight security place which even today nobody is allowed, not even the President.

Mr. Cooper writes that President Eisenhower had a previously arranged meeting with an ET on2/20/1954 at MUTOC now known as the Edwards Air Force Base in Florida. The President had planned a vacation at Palm Springs, FL for the meeting, and his excuse was that he was visiting his dentist. The main ET entity was given the name of Krill. The meeting was confirmed by a letter from Gerald Light a metaphysical researcher who was present at the meeting. The book lists the names of the US officials present at the meeting. In the agreement, the E.Ts would furnish us with advanced technology, and we in turn would allow the E.Ts to perform medical and genetic research on abducted humans with the stipulation that no harm would be inflicted upon them, and that they would not have any memory of the event. They would also be allowed to build underground bases under Indian reservations in Utah, Colorado, New Mexico and Arizona.18
Several attempts were made on Cooper's Life but he miraculously survived. In the second attempt he lost a leg, and sometime later he was found dead, with a bullet in his head.

148

Paul T. Hellyer, former Minister of Defense and former Acting Prime Minister of Canada delivered in Washington DC a disturbing message to the American people, recorded in March 2015. In this message Hellyer warns about the sinister shadow government which deliberately keeps ninety five percent of the population in the dark. He confirms that the Roswell crash was true, and that a high officer of his government Robert Smith wrote a highly classified document about this incident. The Air Force version of the weather balloon was a fabrication and a lie, part of the disinformation program.

He also discussed several other illegal, anti-constitutional activities of this criminal group.

The Bulgarian government announced to the media in 2000 that aliens already exist on earth and that they were in contact with them. Lachezar Filipov, deputy director of the Research institute of the Bulgarian Academy of Science said "Aliens are currently all around us and are watching us all the time."

In short, we have made ET contact for a millennia, but the secret has been well hidden. More recently, since the creation of nuclear weapons, UFO activities have increased. Every country that has nuclear weapons has experienced instances where after being visited by UFOs their power has been rendered ineffective. This has been well documented.

One of the individuals who has had significant experience dealing with ETs is Sixto Paz-Wells, a Peruvian researcher who at an early age made the first contact with ET civilizations. After doing some ESP experiments, through automatic writing he was given an appointment to witness a UFO landing. He was a teenager at that point and invited some of his friends for that event. They all were able to see the UFO, and after this first experience he has accumulated vast information about life in other planets. He has visited Ganymede, the largest of Jupiter's moons and has taken note on how they produced their food, what their dwellings look like, and other aspect of life in that moon. In one of these episodes he invited a well-known writer in Spain JJ Benitez who later wrote a book on UFOs.

Sixto, while living in Florida spoke about his experiences with UFOs, but the authorities did not like what he was doing and confiscated his passport. He was banned from entering the US for twenty years, despite the fact that his mother was an American.

He holds regular E.T meetings in Mexico and other countries and his meetings are open to members of the press, who have documented the encounters with many photographs and videotapes, available online.

There is significant information on E.T activity in our planet, and today anyone who does not believe in the reality of UFOs and ET life, is simply uninformed. One does not have to believe anymore, you just know the truth or you don't.

Chapter 11

The New World

Before considering what the New World would
be like, we must describe the world we are
experiencing at present. We really do not
know who we are. We have been lead to
believe that we are insignificant, small,
and frail, but this is far from the truth.
We live in a world where only a minority of
the population have enough to eat and
relatively secure life style. The rest
struggle to keep their heads above water.
We have polluted the water in our rivers and
oceans, the air we breathe is contaminated,
the foods we eat have been genetically
engineered, full of poisonous preservatives
and pesticides and the meat we eat is loaded
with antibiotics and hormones.
We have bought deeply into the principle of
insufficiency, and so, since there is not
enough, we fight for our resources, entire
countries go to war for their oil, their
land and their supplies.
We are all really One, but we think we are
separated and not equal. Such sense of
isolation and disconnection is what makes us
feel small, powerless and insignificant. We
discriminate against other races, other
creeds, our religions, pretend to be the
only ones and our history is full of wars

between religions, political philosophies, political parties and our thirst for power and dominion seems to have no limit. Poverty and disease are a common denominator. Because of the principle of separation, we as a country may feel superior to other countries. We have more weapons, more wealth, so we feel right in subjugating other nations into submission. Western governments give 'aid' to poor countries, while the big corporations they own and control exploit those countries and bleed them dry of far more wealth than they ever receive in aid. The concept of brotherhood seems foreign and impractical to most of us.

The overwhelming majority of us don't realize that that we are controlled and enslaved by the elite, which is a group of the richest and most influential families who operate through secret societies in great secrecy, and behind the scenes. Their aim is to establish the "New World Order" in which we will have one world government, a fascist state, a global version of Nazi Germany, in which the people will be prisoners of a dictatorship with suppression of the most fundamental freedoms and total control and surveillance. The aim is also to have one religion (theirs),one monetary unit with one Central bank, one global military, one global medical system, and of course one educational system over

153

which they would have total control. Nobody
will be allowed to have any property, so the
Central Government should give us what we
need (which is really rationing). The
question may be asked: If we have one global
military, there should be no one to fight,
why an army? It is necessary to insure
complete submission, to make sure nobody
rebels against the system, and make sure
everyone conforms to their dictated norms,
keeping everyone under constant
surveillance. The plan includes removing
children from the influence of their
parents, to break up the family unit, and
teach children to worship the state.
Dr. Greer calls this elite group Murder Inc.
These bloodlines consider themselves to be
superior to the rest of us. They believe
that they are the descendants of a more
advanced civilization known as the Anunnaki
that came to earth several thousand years
ago, and related to what is call in the
Bible "the Fallen Angels." They believe they
were the original pharaohs, kings, monarchs,
emperors and rulers of the world, so, they
feel justified in their attempts to control
and subjugate us.

Documents, statements and writings that have
emerged over the years make it very clear
that one of the aims of this elite group is
to reduce the population to no more than 500
million! That is six billion fewer than at

present.
They have total control over the banking system which they own. This system was created to exploit society with loans, mortgages and credit cards which have to be re-paid with big interests and fees, making us slaves and dependent on the establishment, while the Global Elite amass large amounts of wealth, and the middle class buried in great debt, struggle to cope with the demands of life needs.

The elite created and control the Federal Reserve, own the oil industry, the powerful pharma cartel, and most of the large international big corporations. We may see different names in corporations, organizations and companies, but they are ultimately owned and controlled by the very few. They control the international politics, the global news media, and the educational system. The mass media, contrary to what they lead us to believe, do not have free speech, and must fit into precise formulated scripts.
Modern education could be accurately called a brain washing system that is geared towards enhancement of their plans and agenda. We are given false information international politics, and we cannot see beyond the scope of what they have programmed us to believe, since they control the entire educational system and the media.

This elite group control science and technologies and use scientific achievements for their benefit. Serious and well-meaning researchers who create technologies to better our world are systematically suppressed.

Writer and researcher David Wilcock in his book "The Source Field" writes about a meeting he had with NASA astronaut Dr. Brian O'Leary in Zurich, Switzerland while they were both speakers at a conference. O'Leary gave him a significant amount of information regarding free energy devices that had been invented again and again but were invariably suppressed by powerful corporations. He said that some researchers are bought off, others threatened into submission, and others die under strange circumstances. He then gave Wilcock examples of how two known leading free energy researchers were murdered.

We know that technology exist, since the early 40's to produce free energy and eliminate our dependence on fossil fuels. This technology would eliminate poverty and would avoid further pollution, but the secret has been kept from us, so that the huge oil and coal industry continue to create trillions in profit. They own the right conservative wing as well as the left liberal networks. This seems highly contradictory, but it is not. This is just part of the long term plan for total control.

They orchestrated World War I and II, they put Hitler in power, after attempts to create a totalitarian dictatorship in US in 1915 failed. During World War II they funded both sides of the war for financial gain and they provided the weapons to both.

This is not conspiracy theory. We see their plans being implemented gradually. They are behind every monetary crisis and every revolution. The UN (United Nations) over which they have total control, was created as a part of the plan, giving us the illusion of a peace keeping body to protect and represent us, but is in reality no more than a large control union.

The idea of one government system is behind the European Union and The African Union. There have been attempts to create a Latin American Union as well. The notion of one monetary system is behind the creation of the Euro, and there are reports which indicate that they plan to replace the US and Canadian dollar as well as the Mexican peso with the Amero, a working title for the new currency for the North American Union. National currencies are rapidly disappearing to be replaced by collective currencies. Their aim is to eventually create a single electronic world currency with a cashless system which they can easily manipulate and control.

Paul T. Hellyer, ex-Defense Minister of Canada mentioned earlier, aware of the corrupted activities of this shadowy group wrote a book "Money Mafia," in which he exposes the illegal and anti-constitutional activities of this group which has enslaved us, and gives suggestions as to what can be done to reverse the process and give the people back their basic human rights.

David Icke is a British researcher and author of several books exposing the activities of this elite. His books give us a chilling description of the secret activities carried out by this group to implement their sinister agenda.
He writes about how the WHO (World Health Organization) was created by the Rothschild and the Rockefeller families to dictate global health policy.
The Rothschild- Rockefeller networks created medical associations such as the BMA (British Medical Association), to control medicine and the medical profession. The AMA (American Medical Association) was established in 1847, and immediately set up to control medical schools supported by the Rockefeller family and the Illuminati Carnegie Foundation.
They opposed acupuncture, homeopathic medicine and any other method of alternative medicine for as long as they could.
Eventually they had to give in and allow

them to operate.

Big pharma which they own, is a multibillion industry. The top ten drug companies make more money in profits than the rest of the Fortune 500 combined. Figures by the Center for Responsive Politics, the Campaigning Financial Institute and the Center for Public Integrity revealed that in 2004, $158 million was spent by drug companies to lobby the US Federal Government, $17 million of which was for political campaigns.

Big pharma has 1,300 lobbyists in Washington DC alone. That is more than two for each member of congress.

They spend nearly $19 billion a year bribing and influencing physicians to prescribe their expensive drugs. In my years of practicing medicine I witnessed their systematic efforts to influence the medical establishment. In my group practice alone, at least twice a week a drug representative brought free lunch for all the staff, in attempts to push their products.

Today, on TV you cannot watch most programs without being bombarded every five minutes or so, with ads of expensive chemotherapy and other drugs.

Chemotherapy drugs are advertised as prolonging life, but they are the number one destroyer of the immune system. They have their place in certain forms of cancer, and no doubt they have been helpful, but they are terribly abused. They are very expensive and this is one of the reasons for the big push and pressure on the medical community to use them.

I remember a conference sponsored by a well-known drug company, in which the point was made that the chemotherapy product they were presenting, had shown to prolong life by two to three months! The side effects of the drug were very significant, patients developed nausea, vomiting and other symptoms. At the end of the presentation, I had to stand up and ask if this drug was really prolonging life, or was it not prolonging death? The quality of life of people on this chemotherapy could hardly be called life. All this suffering for two or three months of misery! Many doctors in the audience were in agreement, and needless to say, I became very unpopular with the company which manufactured the drug, and was never invited again to any of their presentations.
People on chemotherapy have their immune systems destroyed, making them more susceptible to any type of infection, and of course they develop many adverse reactions.
I find it incredible that drugs in the US are so expensive. You can buy the same drugs by the same manufacturers, in Canada and in Mexico for a small fraction of the cost. In my practice, very frequently I witnessed the difficulty many patients who live on social

security experience with the cost of their
drugs, frequently having to balance between
buying the drugs and buying food.
Politicians are unable to change the system
because many of them when they come to
office are already mortgaged by the big
contributors to their campaigns. You don't
bite the hand that feeds you, so they will
never vote for anything that would not be in
the best interest of the big pockets of the
corporations that finance their campaigns.
With few exceptions, their main concerns is
being re-elected, so they will agree with
whoever is in power, regardless of how they
really feel and think about the issues. And
the sad thing is that we think they are
there to represent our best interests.

In one of David Icke's recent books,
"Humanity, Get Off Your Knees," he discusses
how this elite group's agenda of reducing
the population to no more than 500 million,
is operating in combination with big pharma,
creating in the laboratory different kinds
of flu, and mandatory vaccinations, which
are killing thousands.

In June 10, 2009 Austrian journalist Jane
Burgermeister announced in 2009 that she had
filed criminal charges with the FBI against
the World Health Organization, the United
Nations, David Rockefeller, George Soros,
Barack Obama and others over a plot she
uncovered to cull the population with a

deadly vaccine. She said that the bird flu and swine flu had been developed in the laboratory and released to the public with aim of mass murder through vaccination. Her filed document was called Bioterrorism Evidence for Political Gain.

Dr. Leonard Horowitz is perhaps the world's most celebrated pharmaceutical industry whistleblower. A doctor, and leading humanitarian, author of 17 books, explains how the AIDS virus was deliberately created through Hepatitis B vaccinations. He gives a list of many diseases caused by vaccinations and explains that the reason for sky rocketing increase in autism and Alzheimer's has to do with mandatory vaccinations. This has also been confirmed by many other sources.
They are destroying the immune system through the use of food additives, pesticides and food manipulation. We also know that sperm counts have dropped by one third since 1989 and by 50 percent in the last fifty years.
The research about food additives was published in the prestigious medical journal Lancet, in 3-9 Nov, 2007. It revealed that there is a clear link between food additives and hyperactive behavior in children.
Scientists from the University of Southampton in England conducted a research on nearly 300 three-year old and eight-year

old children, none of which suffered from any hyperactivity disorder.

They drank a mixture of additives that reflected the average daily additive intake of a British child, and afterward they were observed boisterous behavior and inability to concentrate. The eight- year olds were unable to complete a fifteen minute computer exercise.

It now appears that no such thing as ADD (Attention Deficit Disorder) exists, except for what is produced by food additives, and too many hours in front of the TV. This was a hoax spread by the big pharma to justify the use of more drugs. ADD It has been treated with Ritalin and other mind altering drugs.

Studies in England and Australia have shown that six capsules a day of fish oil can improve these children's behavior and are more effective than drugs.

The Georgia Guidestones, is a large granite monument erected in 1980 in Elbert County, in the state of Georgia in the United States. A set of ten guidelines is inscribed on the structure in eight modern languages. This massive structure which is sometimes referred to as the "American Stonehenge," was built and commissioned by a man using the pseudonym Robert C. Christian. He explained that he represented a group which had been planning the guide stones for 20 years.

It is believed that the group to which he was referring to was the Global New World Order, Illuminati or the Cabal as it is also called, because the guidelines are consistent with the aim of reducing the population to no more than 500 million, and other mandates which are identical to the aims of this secret society.

Icke, and other researchers discuss many other methods the Elite group is employing to reduce the population. One effective method is through war.

They are working hard to bring about World War III involving North America, Europe, Russia, and China.

The idea is to create global conflict that would lead to the imposition of global world government with one military system to "keep this from happening again."

They have already started the program of implanting coated microchips, frequently through small needles used with vaccinations and placed under the skin. Their plan is to eventually implant them in every person, which will tie us into a master computer that would track down anyone at any time. Their pretext is that if we are all microchipped, it would be easy for a hospital or any medical facility to immediately go through the entire medical history to expedite treatment without delay, and that it would be easier to locate missing persons. In reality the only purpose behind such program is to have total control over the individual.

Unbelievable as it may sound, it is true. It is difficult to believe that a small group would have so much power, and be able to carry out such atrocities. You would not do it, I would not do it, but they do. Icke writes that these bloodlines have different DNA, and that they do not have empathy, so, they can kill hundreds of people and not feel bad at all. They are just working on their agenda and doing their job.

We, not knowingly, have become like obedient sheep, believing everything the media tells us, abiding by every mandate of those in power, following their dictates without question, disconnected, feeling powerless, and victims of a world we cannot control. There are other courageous people who have been telling us the truth, and unmasking the corruption of those secret societies that compose the tyrannical group. People like Stephen Greer, David Wilcock, Leonard Horowitz and many others have been working tirelessly to make us aware of the deep state of enslavement in which we live, and to make us wake up from our slumber, get off our knees and get our heads out from under the sand.

These facts when known, makes our heads shake in amazement and disbelief. We are "All That Is," What are doing on our knees?

We are "all power" disguised as sheep, and we need to wake up from our deep trance and stop being abused and building a police state for our own children and grandchildren.

It is the true that the elite have been manipulating us, but it is us, the people who choose to play it out on their behalf. If enough people wake up, come together, unmask the perpetrators and refuse to follow their commands, the abuse cannot continue, the perpetrators will become ineffective, unable to continue to lie to us and will be exposed for what they truly are behind the mask of secret societies.

Fortunately the world is awakening. Through awakening, we can change the vibrational frequency of the planet. Love is required as a necessary building block for a now world. When we wake up from our sleep, we will be responsible for our destiny, and we will no longer tolerate the subjugation we have been under for so long. No longer will we be supportive of a system that has enslave us. The old system will be obsolete.

All over the world we are seeing changes at all levels, and as these changes continue we will eventually have The New World, (not the New World Order), one world in which everyone is awake, in which we realize that we are all One, a world in which we have made open contact with our brothers and sisters throughout the universe in peace and harmony with mutual cooperation and good will. We will no longer find comfort in being blind. Our cities will evolve into celestial appearing structures, with a light of their own. Everything will have a life manifesting divine qualities in every aspect of life. We will interact with every galactic civilization, and with angelic and celestial beings. This will be indeed an exciting world.

We will be the UFOs of less advanced civilizations, which we will approach with caution and love, not wanting to interfere with their evolution and destiny but to assist them in their development, just as we were assisted by highly developed societies in ours.

In this new world there will not be competition but cooperation. Religions will be based in truth and love not in fear and intolerance. In the new world we all will have reached self-realization that is the knowledge that we and God are one. We will know that God becomes everything and is everything, because there is nothing to make anything else from. We will learn that God is in every atom, every subatomic particle which makes our world.

Having reached this degree of realization, there could not be any possible wars, we will be truly brothers and sisters in mutual cooperation and love. Disease and poverty will be only mentioned in history books. We could look back to a painful history that taught us the necessary lessons to be what we will have become.

As it is the case in other presently advanced civilizations, we will no longer need technology, because we will have discovered that consciousness can create anything will need. ''This will be indeed Heaven on Earth!

Bibliography

1-Talbot, Michael, The Holographic Universe. Harper Collins Publishing, 1992

2-Strindberg, August Legends, as Quoted in Colin Wilson, The Occult (New York: Vintage Books, 1973, p56,57.

3-Lipton, Bruce, The Biology of Belief. Hay House Inc. First Edition 2015, second, 2016

4-Osho, Learning to silence the Mind, St Martin's Griffin, N.Y. 1912

5-Goldsmith Joel, Parenthesis in Eternity, Harper San Francisco 1963.

6-Garfield Charles A. Peak Performance (New York: Warner Books, 1984, p.16

7-Neville, The Power of Imagination, Penguin, 2015

8-Talbot Michael, The Holographic Universe, Harper Collins Publishers 1992

9-Mason A. A case of Congenital Ichthyosiform British Medical Journal 2; 1952, p 422-23

10-Roberts Jane, Seth Speaks Amber-Allen Publishing New World Library, 1972

11-Powell, A.E., The Astral Body Theosophical Class Series, Quest 1972

12-Baker Douglas, Life After Death Claregate College, Potters Bar, Hertz, England, 1981

13-Whitton Joel, Life between Life, New York: Doubleday, 1986, pp116.

14-Nealson Kenneth, Popular Mechanics, July 1999, p 66

15-Laird, Bob, USA Today Life section, March 16, 2001, p 1

16-Cooper Gordon, July 14,1968 Letter to the UN published in Above Top-secret (New York)

17-Greer Steven, Video Conference Nov 2015

18-Cooper, William, Behold a Pale Horse, Light Technology Publishing, 1992

83468780R00102

Made in the USA
Middletown, DE
12 August 2018